UNDERSTANDING DRUGS

Alcohol

TITLES IN THE *UNDERSTANDING DRUGS* SERIES

UNDERSTANDING DRUGS

BAKER COLLEGE OF
CLINTON TWP. LIBRARY

Alcohol

JUSTIN T. GASS, PH.D.

CONSULTING EDITOR
DAVID J. TRIGGLE, PH.D.
University Professor
School of Pharmacy and Pharmaceutical Sciences
State University of New York at Buffalo

CHELSEA HOUSE
PUBLISHERS
An imprint of Infobase Publishing

Chelsea House
An imprint of Infobase Publishing
132 West 31st Street
New York NY 10001

Library of Congress Cataloging-in-Publication Data

Gass, Justin T.
  Alcohol / Justin T. Gass ; consulting editor, David J. Triggle.
    p. cm. — (Understanding drugs)
  Includes bibliographical references and index.
  ISBN-13: 978-1-60413-529-9 (hardcover : alk. paper)
  ISBN-10: 1-60413-529-8 (hardcover : alk. paper)   1. Alcoholism—Juvenile
    literature.   2. Alcohol—Physiological effect—Juvenile literature.   3. Drinking of
    alcoholic beverages—Juvenile literature.   I. Title.   II. Series.
  HV5066.G37 2010
  362.292—dc22
                                                              2010010047

Chelsea House books are available at special discounts when purchased in bulk quantities for businesses, associations, institutions, or sales promotions. Please call our Special Sales Department in New York at (212) 967-8800 or (800) 322-8755.

You can find Chelsea House on the World Wide Web at
http://www.chelseahouse.com

Text design by Kerry Casey
Cover design by Alicia Post
Composition by Newgen
Cover printed by Bang Printing, Brainerd, Minn.
Book printed and bound by Bang Printing, Brainerd, Minn.
Date printed: September 2010
Printed in the United States of America

10 9 8 7 6 5 4 3 2 1

This book is printed on acid-free paper.

All links and Web addresses were checked and verified to be correct at the time of publication. Because of the dynamic nature of the Web, some addresses and links may have changed since publication and may no longer be valid.

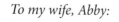

To my wife, Abby:
Thank you for everything that you do for me. You mean the world to me
and I am eternally grateful for having you in my life.

Contents

foreword

THE USE AND ABUSE OF DRUGS

For thousands of years, humans have used a variety of sources with which to cure their ills, cast out devils, promote their well-being, relieve their misery, and control their fertility. Until the beginning of the twentieth century, the agents used were all of natural origin, including many derived from plants as well as elements such as antimony, sulfur, mercury, and arsenic. The sixteenth-century alchemist and physician Paracelsus used mercury and arsenic in his treatment of syphilis, worms, and other diseases that were common at that time; his cure rates, however, remain unknown. Many drugs used today have their origins in natural products. Antimony derivatives, for example, are used in the treatment of the nasty tropical disease leishmaniasis. These plant-derived products represent molecules that have been "forged in the crucible of evolution" and continue to supply the scientist with molecular scaffolds for new drug development.

Our story of modern drug discovery may be considered to start with the German physician and scientist Paul Ehrlich, often called the father of chemotherapy. Born in 1854, Ehrlich became interested in the ways in which synthetic dyes, then becoming a major product of the German fine chemical industry, could selectively stain certain tissues and components of cells. He reasoned that such dyes might form the basis for drugs that could interact selectively with diseased or foreign cells and organisms. One of Ehrlich's early successes was development of the arsenical "606"—patented under the name *Salvarsan*—as a treatment for syphilis. Ehrlich's goal was to create a "magic bullet," a drug that would target only the diseased cell or the invading disease-causing organism and have no effect on healthy cells and tissues. In this he was not successful, but his great research did lay the groundwork for the successes of the twentieth century, including the discovery of the sulfonamides and the antibiotic penicillin. The latter agent saved countless lives during World War II. Ehrlich, like many scientists, was an optimist. On the eve of World War I, he wrote, "Now that the liability to, and danger of, disease are to a large extent circumscribed—the efforts of chemotherapeutics are directed as far as possible to fill up the gaps left in this ring." As we shall see in the pages of this volume, it is neither the first nor the last time that science has proclaimed its victory over nature, only to have to see this optimism dashed in the light of some freshly emerging infection.

From these advances, however, has come the vast array of drugs that are available to the modern physician. We are increasingly close to Ehrlich's magic bullet: Drugs can now target very specific molecular defects in a number of cancers, and doctors today have the ability to investigate the human genome to more effectively match the drug and the patient. In the next one to two decades, it is almost certain that the cost of "reading" an individual genome will be sufficiently cheap that, at least in the developed world, such personalized medicines will become the norm. The development of such drugs, however, is extremely costly and raises significant social issues, including equity in the delivery of medical treatment.

The twenty-first century will continue to produce major advances in medicines and medicine delivery. Nature is, however, a resilient foe. Diseases and organisms develop resistance to existing drugs, and new drugs must constantly be developed. (This is particularly true for anti-infective and anticancer agents.) Additionally, new and more lethal forms of existing infectious diseases can develop rapidly. With the ease of global travel, these can spread from Timbuktu to Toledo in less than 24 hours and become pandemics. Hence the current concerns with avian flu. Also, diseases that have previously been dormant or geographically circumscribed may suddenly break out worldwide. (Imagine, for example, a worldwide pandemic of Ebola disease, with public health agencies totally overwhelmed.) Finally, there are serious concerns regarding the possibility of man-made epidemics occurring through the deliberate or accidental spread of disease agents—including manufactured agents, such as smallpox with enhanced lethality. It is therefore imperative that the search for new medicines continue.

All of us at some time in our life will take a medicine, even if it is only aspirin for a headache or to reduce cosmetic defects. For some individuals, drug use will be constant throughout life. As we age, we will likely be exposed to a variety of medications—from childhood vaccines to drugs to relieve pain caused by a terminal disease. It is not easy to get accurate and understandable information about the drugs that we consume to treat diseases and disorders. There are, of course, highly specialized volumes aimed at medical or scientific professionals. These, however, demand a sophisticated knowledge base and experience to be comprehended. Advertising on television is widely available but provides only fleeting information, usually about only a single drug and designed to market rather than inform. The intent of this series of books, **Understanding Drugs**, is to provide the lay reader with intelligent, readable, and accurate descriptions of drugs, why and how they are used, their limitations, their side effects, and their future. The series will discuss both *"treatment drugs"*—typically, but not exclusively, prescription drugs, that have well-established criteria of both efficacy and safety—and *"drugs of abuse,"* agents that have pronounced pharmacological and physiological effects but that are, for a variety of reasons, not to be considered for therapeutic purposes. It is our hope that these books will provide readers with sufficient information to satisfy their immediate needs and to serve as an adequate base for further investigation and for asking intelligent questions of health care providers.

—David J. Triggle, Ph.D.
University Professor
School of Pharmacy and Pharmaceutical Sciences
State University of New York at Buffalo

1
Introduction and Overview

Travis never understood the buzz around using alcohol. He couldn't comprehend how it was glorified in college and advertising yet still cause significant harm to users including his alcoholic grandfather. Travis had many friends who used alcohol on a regular basis and never had problems with it. However, before his grandfather died, he discovered how addiction to alcohol could be lethal. He watched as his grandfather suffered from memory loss, seizures, and hallucinations in the few months before his death. Travis often wondered why alcohol was legal even when it could cause such severe damage to a user and his or her family. Beer commercials on television only describe the pleasurable effects of alcohol, but Travis learned firsthand that this drug also has an ugly side.

Alcohol is a drug. Some people may not regard it as a *dangerous* one, but it is a drug nonetheless. When considering the influence alcohol has had in our society, it can easily be seen as the Dr. Jekyll and Mr. Hyde of the drug scene. Alcohol's effects can be portrayed as a "split personality" that produces both highly positive feelings and extremely negative consequences.

THE DUAL EFFECTS OF ALCOHOL

The way society views **alcohol** depends on how it is used. For instance, alcohol is present at the majority of celebratory events. One often celebrates with alcohol at parties, weddings, family gatherings, and holidays. Alcohol is also

Figure 1.1 Alcohol is used at many social gatherings to increase interactions among guests. (© Shutterstock)

present in some religious ceremonies and sacred holidays. Some cultures only use alcohol occasionally, whereas others drink it nightly at the dinner table.[1]

Alcohol is used in these situations mainly for the beneficial effects it has in social situations. Alcohol acts as a "social lubricant" in situations when it is helpful to be more relaxed and talkative. The ability of alcohol to increase sociality is due to its effects on the brain. Alcohol "disinhibits" or "releases the brake" that normally controls our actions and impulses. Moderate amounts of alcohol relieve the anxiety and nervousness that may accompany social situations. This allows us to feel more relaxed and to converse more easily with others. These effects of alcohol are consistent with its Dr. Jekyll personality.

The so-called social effects of alcohol are reinforced by its portrayal in the media. Each day millions of people in the United States are confronted with alcohol-related advertising on television, in film, in magazines, and on billboards. Although the influence that these advertisements have on overall alcohol consumption is debatable, the "safe" image of alcohol that is abundant in these media can be influential nonetheless.

On the other hand, excessive intake or chronic use of alcohol can reveal the Mr. Hyde characteristics of the drug. Alcohol is a depressant drug, meaning that it slows down activity of the brain and body. Therefore, moderate and high levels of use can result in drastic deficits in an individual's reaction time, coordination, sensory perception, and cognition. In other words, alcohol intoxication can decrease your hand-eye coordination, decrease visual ability, disrupt memory formation, cause blackouts, and increase dangerous, impulsive behavior.

Additionally, repeated use of alcohol can result in **withdrawal symptoms** when the user attempts to stop consumption. Many drugs cause withdrawal symptoms when a person stops using them. Even prescription and over-the-counter drugs can cause such symptoms, but they are generally mild and go away after a short period of time without much damage to the user. However, the withdrawal symptoms associated with alcohol and other abused drugs are often more severe and can cause significant distress.

Generally speaking, withdrawal symptoms are the opposite of the drug's initial effects on the body. For instance, alcohol is used to produce feelings of relaxation and calmness and the withdrawal effects consist of **anxiety** and restlessness. The severity of alcohol withdrawal symptoms depend on several factors such as the amount of alcohol ingested and the length of use and the age and genetic blueprint of the user. Moderate use can result in mild withdrawal symptoms—such as increased restlessness, anxiety, and difficulty sleeping. With extended periods of use or larger amounts of alcohol ingestion, the withdrawal effects can become as severe as **disorientation, convulsions**, vivid **hallucinations**, and a loss of contact with reality. One potential result of alcohol withdrawal, but that is not common among other drugs of abuse, is death.

IS ALL ALCOHOL THE SAME?

Where did alcohol come from? It has been around for quite some time. In the mid-1600s, the term "alcohol" was used to describe a fine-powdered substance, similar to makeup, which was used to darken the eyebrows. Since this word originally referred to a very fine powder, the term "alcohol" was borrowed and used to describe highly purified liquids containing this drug.[2] Today alcohol is a chemical that refers to a class of substances that contains a hydroxyl group that is bound to a carbon atom—many forms of alcohol are not consumed.

The type of alcohol that is found in alcoholic beverages is known as **ethanol**, or ethyl alcohol. While other chemicals in this class can produce similar effects to ethanol, they are not meant for consumption and can be very harmful if used as a beverage. For instance rubbing alcohol (**isopropyl** alcohol) is often used for cleaning purposes. If ingested, rubbing alcohol is twice as toxic as ethanol and can result in vomiting, nausea, headaches, and dizziness. **Methanol**, also known as wood alcohol, is a chemical that has a similar odor to ethanol but is sweeter. It is commonly used as a solvent for laboratory use, as fuel, and in the production of woods and paints. Methanol is extremely toxic and, if ingested in very small amounts, can cause blindness.

Ethanol is a colorless liquid that is formed by a naturally occurring reaction known as **fermentation**. This process is used in the production of alcohol as a beverage. Fermentation occurs when sugars (such as glucose) are converted into energy. During this conversion, both alcohol and carbon dioxide are produced. Interestingly, the ethanol produced is actually a waste product of this reaction. The term *alcohol* refers to all chemicals in this class; however, the remainder of this book will use the term to refer to ethanol or the type ingested for intoxication.

"DIFFERENT DRINKS, DIFFERENT ALCOHOL CONTENT"

There are numerous alcoholic beverages available to be consumed. A few of the most common classes include beers, wines, and distilled beverages. These products are not all produced in the same manner. Usually the type of materials used in the production of the alcohol determines how it will be classified. **Beer**, for instance, is produced from barley, wheat, or other materials that contain starch. Facilities known as **breweries** are responsible for adding flavor to the beer by adding hops and aging (storing) it for a specified amount of time. Beers usually contain about 3% to 6% alcohol by volume depending on the brand name and the specific fermentation process. When someone ferments grapes or grape juice, the result is **wine** instead of beer. Grapes are crushed and then fermented to produce the alcohol necessary for the wine. Skins and pulp are separated from the grapes in the preparation of white wine, whereas the skins are retained in the fermentation of red wine. Like beer, the taste of wine can be aged to enhance the flavor. The most common types of wine (red, white, and rosé) have approximately 12% alcohol, while some port wines may contain up to 20% alcohol by volume. Products, such as whisky and scotch, that have an alcoholic content above 12% must be made through the process of distillation.

The user can determine the amount of alcohol in a drink by its percentage of alcohol or by its "proof." The first, which is often used by beers and wines, is the alcohol content that is indicated on the label of the bottle. For instance, beers often have the words "contains 6% alcohol" clearly written on the label. Other alcoholic mixtures, such as the ones often mixed with other drinks, refer to the amount of alcohol as "proof." This term originated from the British navy. Sailors were often given a ration of rum each day as part of their payment. Obviously, the navy had to purchase large amounts of rum, and to determine that the alcohol content had not been watered down, it was mixed with gunpowder and then ignited. If the mixture

Figure 1.2 All alcoholic drinks should contain a label that indicates the amount of alcohol in the beverage. *(© Alamy)*

contained too much water it would not burn. If the mixture did burn, it provided "proof" that the rum did indeed have an adequate amount of alcohol. Those formulations of rum were considered "100 degrees proof." It was later determined that the mixtures that burned contained approximately 50% alcohol. Thus, an alcohol mixture that is 100 proof contains 50% alcohol.

WHY NOT JUST CALL IT ALCOHOL?

Abused drugs are often known best by slang names. For example, marijuana, cocaine, and heroin are known as the slang terminology *weed, blow,* and *smack,* respectively. Similarly, many names refer to alcoholic beverages— *booze, canned heat, brew, beverage, hooch, jack, juice, hard stuff,* and *sauce.* Additionally, there are slang terms for being intoxicated with alcohol. These include *wasted, plastered, tanked, bombed, tipsy, smashed, loaded, canned, hammered, drunk,* and *blitzed.* This list is by no means exhaustive, and new words for both alcohol and intoxication are created often. The specific terms used depend on factors such as location, sex, and age.

There are numerous alcoholic beverages available today with newer concoctions continually being produced. Beer and wine are the most widely known alcoholic beverages, but other common drinks include rum, vodka,

GENERAL FACTS ABOUT ALCOHOL

Type of drug: Depressant (depresses the central nervous system)

How it is used: Most often taken orally, but also has reportedly been injected for a faster high

Onset of effects: Relatively long, but dependent on amount used and rate of absorption

Duration of effect: Relatively long, but dependent on rate of metabolism

Physical Danger: Moderate to high

Addiction potential: Moderate to high

Figure 1.3 Common alcoholic beverages include beer, wine, vodka, and whiskey. These drinks can be found at local restaurants, supermarkets, and liquor stores.   (© Alamy)

gin, schnapps, cider, tequila, sake, champagne, sherry, liqueur, whiskey, and scotch.

WHAT ALCOHOL DOES TO THE BRAIN AND BODY

Regardless of the name used to describe alcohol or the amount of alcohol in a particular drink, it is still an addictive drug. There are no "safe" amounts of alcohol, and there is not a particular type of alcoholic drink that is more addictive than the others. People can become addicted to alcohol in the form of beer, which contains a small amount of alcohol (3%–6%), or "harder" liquors, such as whiskey, which contain large amounts of alcohol (40%–60%).

How does alcohol affect the body? Most of alcohol's effects occur in the **central nervous system (CNS)**. Once alcohol enters the blood stream, it makes its way to the brain. When it arrives, it can have effects on many areas of the brain, but has the greatest effects on those that control impulsive behavior, memory, and body movements (motor behavior). Alcohol is a depressant drug, which means that it slows down normal information processing in the brain. As a result, these brain areas do not function with the preciseness that is normally required. These alterations reveal themselves as striking changes in the behavior of the user. Long-term use of alcohol can even result in brain damage.

THE CONTROLLED SUBSTANCES ACT

Why are some drugs legal and others not? Essentially, the potential for abuse and a drug's medical usefulness determine how it is classified. In 1970, the U.S. government passed the Controlled Substances Act. This act classified all drugs in five different schedules (classifications). These classifications were based on how medically useful, safe, and addictive a particular drug was. Currently, the Department of Justice and the Department of Health and Human Services determine which drugs are added or removed from the schedules. Although there are currently five schedules, some states have added a sixth classification consisting of substances that are not considered drugs in the typical sense, but are still abused. This would include a substance like toluene—a chemical found in many household cleaning agents that can be inhaled (huffed) to produce intoxication (a high). The drug classification schedules are as follows:[5]

Schedule I. The drug has a high potential for abuse, *no currently accepted* medical use in treatment in the United States, and a lack of accepted safety for use of the drug or other substance under medical supervision. Examples of drugs in this class include heroin, methaqualone, cannabis, and peyote.

Schedule II. The drug has a high potential for abuse, a currently *accepted* medical use in treatment in the United States or a currently accepted medical use with severe restrictions, and abuse of the drug or may lead to severe **psychological** or **physical dependence**. Examples of drugs in the class include morphine, amphetamine, and cocaine (which can be used as a topical anesthetic).

Alcohol is sometimes referred to as a "dirty" drug, meaning that it affects many areas of body in addition to the brain. Alcohol causes the dilation of blood vessels, which causes the body to lose heat. This heat loss, in turn, can slow down several biochemical processes.[3] Alcohol also affects certain hormone levels including those responsible for fluid balance (antidiuretic hormone); as a result, consumption leads to high urine output. Alcohol causes

Schedule III. The drug has a potential for abuse less than the drugs in Schedules I and II, and it has a currently accepted medical use in treatment in the United States. Abuse of the drug or other substances may lead to moderate or low physical dependence or high psychological dependence. Examples of this drug include ketamine, buprenorphine, and anabolic steroids.

Schedule IV. The drug has a low potential for abuse relative to the drugs or other substances in Schedule III. It has a currently *accepted* medical use in treatment in the United States, and abuse of the drug or other substances may lead to limited physical dependence or psychological dependence relative to the drugs or other substances in Schedule III. Examples of drugs in this class include benzodiazepines, chloral hydrate, and some barbiturates.

Schedule V. The drug has a low potential for abuse relative to the drugs or other substances in Schedule IV. It has a currently *accepted* medical use in treatment in the United States, and abuse of the drug or other substances may lead to limited physical dependence or psychological dependence relative to the drugs or other substances in Schedule IV. Examples of drugs in this class include cough suppressants (containing small amounts of codeine) and some opium preparations used to treat diarrhea.

One of the more interesting aspects of this schedule is that two of the most addictive drugs, alcohol and nicotine, are not listed. Although both are addictive and are rarely, if ever, used for medical purposes, neither is included in this list.

cells in the body to dehydrate, or lose water, which increases thirst in the user. Additionally, there are reductions in the sex hormone testosterone.

Alcohol must pass through the mouth, throat, and stomach before it finally gets absorbed into the blood from the small intestine. When alcohol travels through **gastric** areas, it irritates them and causes nausea. Chronic alcohol consumption can cause a buildup of fat and scar tissue in the liver. When the mouth, throat, and liver are exposed to alcohol repeatedly for many years, cancer can develop. Additionally, heavy alcohol use has been shown to increase the risk of heart disease in addicts.

The body isn't the only area that is affected by alcohol; the mind of the user can also change dramatically. For instance, heavy drinking can result in two severe **neurological disorders**. The first, **Wernicke's encephalopathy**, results from alcohol-induced vitamin deficiency. This disease causes a loss of coordination and blurred vision, and it can leave the addict in a permanently confused state. The second, and even more serious disorder is known as **Korsakoff's psychosis** and is characterized by an inability to form new memories. Alcohol abuse can also harm the children of alcoholics. Even though these individuals may never consume any alcohol, the excessive use by their parents can result in torn parent-child relationships or, in the case of children exposed to alcohol in utero, even **Fetal Alcohol Spectrum Disorder (FASD)**. Children with FASD can have facial deformities, growth deficits, and low IQ levels that are consequences of the mother's addiction to alcohol and no fault of their own.

It's easy to concentrate on the most publicized effects of alcohol, particularly those on the body. However, alcohol can affect more than the user; it can also have negative consequences on society. For instance, drinking can lead to traffic-related deaths, assaults on other individuals, vandalism of property, sexual assaults, and noise disturbances. The price that society pays for this behavior is not cheap: Alcoholism is estimated to cost society nearly $180 billion per year.[4]

Even though alcohol is an addictive drug and can produce some of the most serious effects on the body and society, one characteristic distinguishes it from other drugs: It is legal. Alcohol can legally be sold to anyone 21 years of age or older in the United States. The legal drinking age varies around the world but most countries have the limit set between 18 and 21 (although some countries in Europe allow people as young as 16 to purchase it). Possessing or purchasing alcohol under the legal age limit can have serious legal consequences. Underage drinkers can be cited with either civil or criminal offenses that result in revoked privileges and possibly jail time. Additionally, underage drinking can have more pronounced effects on the user's brain because it is not yet fully developed.

IF ALCOHOL IS LEGAL, ISN'T IT SAFE?

One of the major consequences of not having alcohol listed in the schedule of controlled substances is that people are less likely to consider it a dangerous drug. After years of scientific research it is now abundantly clear that alcohol is addictive and can result in striking changes in the brain and behavior of the addict. Nearly 90% of the United States have tried alcohol and half are considered to be current users. The high rate of alcohol use results mainly from the fact that it is legal for adults and widely available for purchase. These two characteristics make the treatment of alcohol addiction even more difficult. Alcohol's legality presents unique issues in dealing with the treatment of addiction. How and why do you have to treat someone who is supposedly addicted to something that is legal? Do these individuals lack the "moral strength" to give up alcohol? Are there other factors than the drug itself that contribute to alcohol addiction? These are some of the topics that this book will explore.

You may wonder why it is important to learn about alcohol's effects on the body. Given alcohol's legality and accessibility, chances are you or someone you know will encounter this drug at celebrations, parties, or friends' homes. It is important to understand both the neurobiological effects and addictive properties of alcohol in case you or a friend becomes interested in using it. Additionally, you may have a family member or know someone who is an alcoholic. The more knowledgeable you are about alcohol addiction, the better you can deal with such a serious disorder.

2
Past and Present Status of Alcohol Use

Abigail had always been tempted to try alcohol. She noticed that many of her friends and family used it on holidays and birthdays. Like most teenagers, Abigail felt that alcohol was "something new" in society and would eventually turn out like every other fad and soon be forgotten. But when she did some research on the topic, Abigail found that alcohol wasn't a modern drug but instead one that has been used for thousands of years. In fact, the drug that was used by her parents just the night before was the same one used by ancient cultures. She was amazed at how something so old could still be so popular today.

Drug addiction, and particularly **alcohol addiction**, has only recently been accepted by society as a disease of the brain instead of a moral dilemma. Whereas it used to be a topic rarely discussed in public, addiction is now widely publicized in movies, magazines, and television. Because of this, many teenagers and young adults may believe that alcohol use is a relatively new fad. However, this is not the case. There is no specific date at which alcohol was first used a drug, but it's apparent that this drug has been used for thousands of years. In fact, it has been suggested that alcohol use began prior to recorded history.[1]

ALCOHOL USE IN ANCIENT CULTURES

One of the earliest uses of alcohol dates back to the Neolithic culture (about 6000 B.C.) when deliberate use of fermentation began. Recipes for the production of a beer-like liquid used in Egypt date back to about 3000 B.C. Some of the earliest methods for preserving beer and wine date back to 2225 B.C. from records made in areas of the Middle East (Iraq). Many groups, including the Egyptians, Babylonians, and Greeks, not only produced alcoholic beverages but also overindulged in it. The Greeks, for example, preached against living in excess and tried to enjoy all things in moderation—except alcoholic beverages. Greeks might have chosen to use alcohol because they believed that intoxication brought individuals closer to their gods. A popular drink among the Greeks was **mead**, a combination of alcohol, honey, and water. Wine was used for celebratory and religious events as it is today. During the rise of the Roman Empire, drinking appears to have been less of a problem than in other cultures. However, after the Roman conquest of the Mediterranean basin, Rome's **temperance**, or moderation, was slowly replaced by the abuse of alcohol. Evidence for this comes from their practices of excessive drinking before meals, drinking games, and vomiting to allow for more consumption of alcohol. Toward the end of the Roman Empire, many Roman citizens, as well as several of the high-ranking emperors, drank heavily. Abuse of alcohol was considered one of the contributing factors that led to the fall of the Roman Empire.[2]

In ancient Egypt, there is evidence of brewing near the beginning of the Egyptian civilization. The Egyptians believed that one of their most important gods, **Osiris**, invented alcohol. One of the necessities of Egyptian life, alcohol was so important that the Egyptians offered it to their gods as a sacrifice. Additionally, Egyptians placed alcoholic beverages in the tombs of the dead so they could take it with them to the afterlife. As is true today, the Egyptians had many different formulations of beer and wine. Even then, individuals in the Egyptian culture suffered from excessive use of alcohol that prompted warnings from leaders about the dangers of overindulgence in this drug.

There is evidence that ancient Babylonians used both beer and wine frequently. Individuals in this culture worshipped a wine goddess, and they also used wine as an offering to their gods. Although there are no reports that explain the extent of alcohol abuse in this culture, there were laws created that specifically mentioned alcohol. This suggests that Babylonians were at least aware of the significance of alcohol use within their culture.

Interestingly, alcohol was also important in ancient China. Records indicate that this civilization produced an alcoholic beverage with a mixture of

Figure 2.1 Alcohol use dates back many years to ancient cultures including the Egyptians. *(© Alamy)*

honey, fruit, and rice. In China, alcohol was considered to be a source of inspiration and an energizer. The Chinese viewed alcohol not as a way to experience pleasure, but as a spiritual substance for religious experiences (rather than at parties and celebrations). Like other ancient cultures, the Chinese used alcohol in memorial ceremonies for loved ones and offered it as a sacrifice to gods and ancestors. Although it was used widely in moderation, there is evidence that some individuals had problems with drinking.

THE MIDDLE AGES DRANK, TOO

During the Middle Ages the popularity of alcohol, especially mead, beer, and wine, grew significantly. Religious monasteries took over the production of wine and beer. It was the job of monks to prepare large quantities of high-quality wines and beers that could be sold to the community. It was during the Middle Ages that a process known as **distillation** was discovered in the production of alcohol. Until this point, the process of fermenting had only allowed the alcohol content in beverages to peak at about 12% (most beers contained about 5% alcohol). The distillation process allowed for the production of beverages such as brandy, which could contain between 40% and 60% alcohol. The advancements made in the production of alcoholic drinks

Figure 2.2 Distillation is a process by which alcohol is heated and the resulting vapors are collected to produce a higher alcohol content than those generated by fermentation.   (© *Photo Researchers, Inc.*)

during this period contributed to an overall increase in the consumption of alcohol and would set the stage for the drinking habits of future societies.[3]

Over the next few hundred years the production and consumption of alcoholic beverages continued to grow and, during the sixteenth century, alcohol consumption remained high. Attitudes toward drinking were still focused on moderate consumption and the benefits associated with occasional use, but people started to notice the negative effects of alcohol. Thus, alcohol began to have a negative reputation—as a substance that could prevent a person from performing his or her job or even from obtaining spiritual enlightenment. Concerns over these damaging effects of ethanol escalated in the coming years and formed the basis of the **Temperance Movement** and Prohibition era in the United States. Despite these concerns, several popular alcoholic beverages were invented during this period including **champagne**, **whiskey**, **rum**, and **gin**.[4]

ATTEMPTS TO STOP ALCOHOL USE IN THE UNITED STATES

In the United States, alcohol had gained significant popularity by the late eighteenth century. Historians report that most Americans of the day drank alcohol and valued it more highly than water. The majority of those people considered it to be a good drink given to them by God. As alcohol use rose to abnormal levels, several groups sought to limit the consumption—a period in the United States known as the Temperance Movement. In the late 1700s and early 1800s several associations were formed that preached moderation of alcohol use. These groups were based on the writings of Benjamin Rush. He was a physician who wrote about the dangers that alcohol abuse can have on both the individual and society. Dr. Rush noticed the association between excessive alcohol use and certain physical disorders such as liver disease, hallucinations, and seizures (which are symptoms currently associated with alcoholism). He also suggested that alcohol abuse leads to damage in the brain areas responsible for morality, and that these changes resulted in antisocial and criminal-like behavior. The Temperance Movement grew in popularity and eventually resulted in the formation of the American Temperance Society. It is important to note that members of the Temperance Movement didn't argue for abstinence from alcohol use, but instead for moderate use. The ideas of this group spread to many parts of the country, and in the mid-1800s, it became almost fashionable for individuals to participate in the movement.[5]

The behavior of "drunks" became even less tolerated as the temperance ideology grew. As a result, the idea of alcohol in moderation evolved into a complete discontinuation of alcohol production, sale, and use. The trend toward abstinence from alcohol began with only minor support, but it quickly gained popularity. In 1851, Maine became the first state to pass a law of **Prohibition**, also known as a "dry period," in which it became illegal to produce or sell alcohol. By 1851, an additional 13 states followed the lead of Maine and enacted laws of prohibition. By 1919, a total of 34 states had legislation that enforced prohibition, 64% of the population lived in a territory that was considered "dry," and more than 100,000 bars were shut down. Eventually, the Unites States Senate proposed an amendment that would bring national Prohibition. The Eighteenth Amendment, effected on January 16, 1920, made it illegal to produce and distribute alcohol within the United States. Although the intent of this amendment was to control the use of alcohol, it did little to suppress the actual consumption of the drug. People still found ways to obtain alcohol, mostly by illegal methods. There were underground clandestine breweries that could make beer and wine. The illegal products were often sold on the black market, and **organized crime** was one of the major providers of alcohol during this period.[6]

The idea of Prohibition was not accepted by everyone, and as the years passed, more and more groups began to oppose this movement. One group in particular was physicians who lobbied for an end to Prohibition. They prescribed alcohol for medicinal purposes, such as the treatment of anxiety. Additionally, organized crime was one of the main (illegal) suppliers of alcohol, so many cities saw an increase in criminal activities during this period. Enforcing Prohibition became quite expensive for taxpayers. The cost of redressing criminal activity, combined with a lack of tax revenue from alcohol sales, made it quite costly to sustain the movement. Alcohol laws were increasingly violated while rates of alcoholism and alcohol-related deaths also increased. All of these factors resulted in the increasing unpopularity of Prohibition in the United States. In 1933, President Franklin Roosevelt signed into law an amendment that allowed the sale of beverages that contained low concentrations of alcohol, such as beer and light wines. Later that year, the Eighteenth Amendment was repealed with the ratification of the Twenty-first

Amendment, which gave each state its own control over the production and distribution of alcohol. Over the next 30 years, more states began to relax their laws on alcohol and eventually, in 1966, the last "dry" state, Mississippi, no longer prohibited alcohol manufacturing or use.

When alcohol had become legal, consumption began to grow steadily. With increased use, the harmful effects of alcohol abuse became more apparent. At the same time, there were significant advances in medical techniques that could be used to study the effects of alcohol on the brain and body. These advancements allowed for more precise examination of alcohol's negative effects. It was found that alcohol can cause serious damage to abusers, and in 1956 alcoholism became officially classified as a disease by the American Medical Association. Soon after, Congress created the National Institute on Alcohol Abuse and Alcoholism (NIAAA). NIAAA is part of the National Institutes of Health (NIH) and provides funds for research related to the study of alcoholism, including the causes, consequences, treatment, and prevention of the disease. This institute funds cutting-edge research on a wide range of scientific disciplines such as neuroscience, genetics, and epidemiology.[7]

Even after the Prohibition era ended and the harmful effects of alcohol surfaced, alcohol use continued to rise and peak in the very late 1970s. Based on the increasing health concerns of alcohol abuse, the public formed organizations (similar to those during the Temperance Movement) that argued for a reduction in alcohol use. One of the most notable such organizations that is still present today is **Mothers Against Drunk Driving (MADD)**. This nonprofit group has a goal to stop drunk driving and to provide support for those who are affected by drunk driving (i.e., the families of victims). A similar organization known as **Students Against Destructive Decisions (SADD)** (formerly Students Against Driving Drunk) was formed soon after to aid in raising awareness of drunk driving fatalities. Groups such as these focus on educating the public about the dangers of drunk driving by calling for strict enforcement of alcohol policies, such as punishment for DUI (driving under the influence) offenders (mandatory jail sentences), penalties for underage consumption (driver's license suspensions), treatment for alcoholism, and support for family members of alcoholics. With more emphasis being placed on alcohol's effects on teenagers, Congress decided in the early 1980s to raise the legal drinking age (which was 18 at the time in some states) to 21. The government developed a unique incentive to persuade certain states to adhere to this new policy. Congress authorized the Transportation Department to withhold funds for the construction and maintenance of federal highways within those states that did not increase their legal drinking age. By 1988, all states had set 21 as the minimum drinking age.[8]

As a result, alcohol use began to decrease slowly in the United States. Data from research studies on alcohol drinking patterns suggest that, although alcohol use may be on a downward trend, consumption tends to go through cycles. Peaks in alcohol use occur every 60 to 70 years. Thus, the recent decrease in consumption doesn't necessarily mean that we have total control over alcohol abuse in the United States. Current lower-than-normal levels of alcohol consumption likely result from an increased concern over its health effects, but a sharp increase in drinking typically follows in this cycle.[9]

CURRENT USE OF ALCOHOL

Comparing alcohol use by year demonstrates a slight decrease in total consumption since the late 1970s. To measure the total amount of alcohol consumed, researchers use statistical terms like "per capita," which means "for each head." Thus, when used to describe alcohol use, it reflects the average amount of alcohol used per person.

Table 2.1 shows per capita alcohol consumption of beer, wine, and distilled beverages (spirits) for the U.S. for individuals age 14 and older. Different states have distinctive patterns of drinking. Table 2.2 shows the average usage by state with the average use of the United States, as a whole, being about 2.27 gallons in 2006.

What could account for the differences in alcohol consumption among these states? One of strongest theories for these different rates suggests that stress and permissive attitudes are major influences on drinking. For instance, cities with high levels of stress (such as big cities) are more likely to approve the use of alcohol to help reduce anxiety levels. Indeed, the cities that were rated as having the highest stress levels were also the ones with the highest rates of alcohol consumption.[10]

Despite a decrease in the total consumption of alcohol over the past few years, a significant percentage of the population in the United States continues to drink large amounts. In 2003, about 120 million people in the United States were considered current users of alcohol. Approximately 54 million

Table 2.1 U.S. per capita alcohol consumption in gallons, age 14 and up[11]				
Year	Beer	Wine	Spirits	Total
2006	1.19	0.37	0.71	2.27
2004	1.20	0.35	0.68	2.23
2002	1.23	0.33	0.65	2.20
2000	1.22	0.31	0.65	2.18
1998	1.22	0.30	0.62	2.14
1996	1.23	0.30	0.63	2.16
1994	1.25	0.28	0.65	2.18
1992	1.29	0.30	0.71	2.30
1990	1.34	0.33	0.77	2.45
1988	1.33	0.36	0.79	2.48
1986	1.34	0.39	0.84	2.58
1984	1.35	0.37	0.94	2.65
1982	1.38	0.36	0.98	2.72
1980	1.38	0.34	1.04	2.76
1978	1.33	0.31	1.07	2.71

Table 2.2 Total per capita alcohol consumption in gallons, by state[12]	
1.99 or below	Alabama, Arkansas, Kansas, Kentucky, New York, North Carolina, Oklahoma, Tennessee, Utah, West Virginia
2.00–2.24	Georgia, Indiana, Iowa, Maryland, Ohio, Pennsylvania, Texas, Virginia, Washington
2.25–2.49	Arizona, California, Connecticut, Illinois, Maine, Minnesota, Mississippi, Missouri, Nebraska, New Jersey, New Mexico, South Carolina, South Dakota
2.50 or over	Alaska, Colorado, Delaware, District of Columbia, Florida, Hawaii, Idaho, Louisiana, Massachusetts, Montana, Nevada, New Hampshire, North Dakota, Oregon, Rhode Island, Vermont, Wisconsin, Wyoming

people took part in binge drinking (five or more drinks on the same occasion at least once during the past month), and approximately 16 million people were considered heavy drinkers (five or more drinks on the same occasion five different times in the last 30 days).[13]

Research studies have shown that about one-third of adults in the United States report that they don't drink any alcohol at all. About two-thirds of the population who do drink alcohol average two to three drinks per day. Nearly half of the alcohol consumed in the United States is used by about 10% of those who drink. There also appear to be differences in alcohol consumption related to ethnicity, geographic location, age, religious practice, and years of education. For instance, whites are more likely to drink than blacks, northerners more than southerners, people who live in large cities more than those in smaller towns, younger adults more than their older counterparts, nonreligious individuals more than religious ones, and those with a college education more than those with a high school education. There are numerous reasons to explain these differences, including socioeconomic status (poorer people may not be able to afford alcohol), religious beliefs (some religions prohibit drinking while others allow it), and expected outcomes of drinking (men drink with the intention of feeling pleasure, whereas women drink more to relieve anxiety).[14]

DRINKING IN COLLEGE

One of the most common sites of alcohol consumption is a college campus. Many adults tell stories of their "drinking days" when they were in college. Drinking alcohol in college has become a tradition in the United States and is now considered part of the college culture. The many movies, books, and television shows that portray college students as heavy drinkers represent a reality on United States campuses. In 2001, the proportion of drinkers was 10% higher among college students between the ages of 18 and 24 than among their noncollegiate counterparts. About 83% of college students drink, and nearly half of those students report drinking five or more drinks on one occasion at least once in the past two weeks (binge drinking). One of the more dangerous types of binge drinking occurs when individuals turn 21 (the legal age to drink). It is common for college students to celebrate this birthday by consuming 21 shots of alcohol or alcoholic beverages.

THE INFLUENCE OF TIME AND CONTEXT ON DRINKING PATTERNS

Much of the data presented in this chapter has focused on the drinking patterns over many years or time periods. But, can specific days of the year (e.g., holidays) or certain environments influence how much a person drinks alcohol? Research on these topics has revealed some very interesting results. For instance, alcohol addiction research studies have shown that when addicts are exposed to environments where they used to drink, such as a bar or certain room in their house, these contexts cause them to crave the drug. This is the reason that many addicts relapse. They are exposed to things in their environment that remind them of alcohol's effects, and when those memories are activated, the addicts have a very difficult time ignoring them.

Alcohol consumption is also influenced by the time of year. When the drinking patterns of college freshman students are analyzed by week, it was found that they drink heavily during the first few weeks of the semester. Their consumption peaks during the weeks of holidays such as Thanksgiving, Christmas, and New Year's Eve. But their drinking peaks aren't limited to holidays, as the highest levels of alcohol consumption typically occurs during the week of spring break. These research studies suggest that, although it may be useful to measure the amount of alcohol consumption by year, it is more informative to track the average number of drinks per week. This data could help schools offer additional treatment options for individuals with a drinking problem during "sensitive" time periods, such as holidays.[15]

Obviously, this method of drinking can cause serious harm to an individual (alcohol poisoning) and even lead to death. Binge drinking also occurs at parties and is sometimes considered a "rite of passage" in college, or for a fraternity or sorority. Furthermore, many of the partygoers are under the legal age to drink. Underage students don't have as many opportunities to drink as legal-age students do, so they try to take advantage of any occasion at which alcohol is present. Thus, this population is more likely to engage in binge drinking at parties when given the chance. Some colleges are considered "dry" and prohibit alcohol on campus, but these rules do little to reduce students' alcohol consumption.[16]

Many students may increase their consumption of alcohol during college, but for most of them, drinking began prior to arriving on campus. By the time these students finish high school, nearly three-quarters of them have had a full drink, a quarter of them have participated in binge drinking, and more than half have already been intoxicated. By demonstrating that many students have experience with alcohol before college, these statistics suggest that college may increase, rather than trigger, a young person's alcohol consumption.[17]

Excessive alcohol use in college has a multitude of effects. First, and most obvious, it can cause direct harm to the individual. Nearly 600,000 students are injured each year while under the influence of alcohol, and more than 150,000 suffer alcohol-related health problems. Nearly a quarter of all college students fall victim to academic consequences that result from their drinking. Damage is not limited to the user, however. Close to 97,000 students are victims of alcohol-related sexual assault or date rape, and nearly 700,000 students are assaulted by another student who is intoxicated.[18]

SUMMARY

This chapter has explored the history of alcohol use by comparing consumption over thousands of years. Although there is not an exact date at which alcohol was introduced, many historians believe that it dates back to before history was recorded. There is evidence for alcohol use in ancient cultures (Egypt, Greece, and Rome) and through the Middle Ages, and it is still one of the most popular drugs used today. Over the years, many forms of alcohol have been introduced, and numerous types remain in our society. Even though we have a great deal of data on the history of alcohol, the ways in which the drug works in our body are only now beginning to be understood.

3
The Neuroscience of Alcohol

Jill was very interested in science as a child. Throughout elementary and high school she took classes that allowed her to participate in scientific experiments. In college, she especially enjoyed physiological psychology. This course allowed her to explore the brain and its many functions. When the topic of drugs and the brain was covered, Jill was astonished to realize that drugs, including alcohol, produce many of their effects in the brain. Alcohol causes a change in the brain chemicals known as neurotransmitters. Because the brain is responsible for almost all of our behaviors, drugs like alcohol can radically affect how we feel and behave.

Most people don't drink alcohol in its natural form. Instead, alcohol is combined with some sort of substance that improves the overall taste of the beverage. This is because many do not like the taste of pure alcohol; it has a very strong, abrasive flavor not unlike rubbing alcohol. Thus, alcohol is usually combined with a sugary or fruity solvent to make it more enjoyable to drink. It is still the alcohol in the beverage, however, that causes intoxication, not the additives.

Alcohol is a compound that has a hydroxyl group (–OH) bound to a carbon atom. There are several different classes of alcohol, but this chapter will focus on ethanol. This type of alcohol has the molecular formula C_2H_5OH, which corresponds to the molecules that comprise it—carbon, hydrogen, and oxygen. Ethanol is commonly abbreviated as EtOH, but this book will use the terms "ethanol" and "alcohol" to refer to the substance that is consumed for intoxication and pleasurable effects.

34

THE STRUCTURES OF THE BRAIN

In order to understand how alcohol affects the body, one must first understand how our bodies are constructed. Drugs must first enter the body, and more specifically, the blood. It is easiest to understand this mechanism by exploring the human body's central nervous system (CNS). Comprised of the brain and spinal cord, the CNS controls most of our actions. The brain has many different structures, and, for the most part, each structure corresponds to a

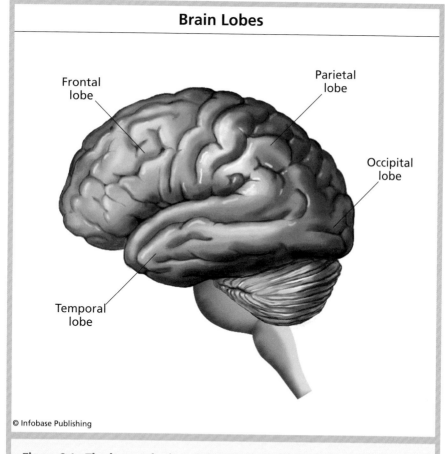

Brain Lobes

Frontal lobe

Parietal lobe

Occipital lobe

Temporal lobe

© Infobase Publishing

Figure 3.1 The human brain consists of four different lobes and each one plays a different role in our behavior. Drugs can have many different effects on this part of our body, but depressant drugs like alcohol produce their effects by slowing down the activity of the brain.

particular function. For instance, there are four different lobes in the brain—the frontal, parietal, temporal, and occipital lobes. The **frontal lobe** is the center for many of our higher-level functions, such as motor ability (movement of body parts), speaking, judgment, decision-making, and impulse control. Electrical stimulation of certain areas in the frontal lobe results in body movements or speech production. The **parietal lobe** is responsible for integrating the vast amount of information that comes from our senses. When an area in this lobe is stimulated, people feel sensations such as objects touching them or an itch. The **temporal lobe** houses the auditory cortex that helps us hear and understand spoken words. When this area is stimulated, people hear things (such as tones) that aren't actually there. Finally, the **occipital lobe** is located at the back of the brain and is responsible for regulating our vision. There are bundles of nerves that travel from the eyes all the way back to the occipital lobe and carry light information from the environment to the brain. Stimulation of these areas causes people to see spots of light.

The brain connects to the spinal cord, which is a long, thin bundle of nerves that relays information to and from the brain with the rest of the body. The brain sends information to the spinal cord that enables muscles to move body parts. On the other hand, sensory receptors in areas outside of the CNS send information back to the brain so they can be interpreted. These signals include feelings of touch, temperature, and even the position of one's arms and legs.

The brain's job isn't limited to regulating body movements and sensations from the environment. The brain is also responsible for a person's feelings and emotions. An area known as the **amygdala** has the job of helping people express feelings of happiness, sadness, and anger, but also allows people to understand the emotions of others. There is also an area of the brain that controls one's ability to feel pleasure or reward. This is the region where drugs of abuse stimulate the brain. In fact, any activity that is found to be rewarding causes activation of this pathway. Drugs, however, "highjack" this reward system and take it over. They produce much larger changes in brain chemicals that underlie pleasure when compared to nondrug rewards like food and water.

NEURONS: THE BUILDING BLOCKS OF THE BRAIN

As soon as the drug reaches the brain, it starts to affect the brains cells. The brain is made up of more than 100 billion cells that are called **neurons**.

Unlike cells that reside outside of the CNS, neurons can communicate with each other. This communication occurs by the transmission of signals from one neuron to the next, and these signals cause the next neuron either to be

WHY ARE THERE DIFFERENT METHODS TO USE DRUGS?

Drugs affect our brains by altering the amount of brain chemicals that are released from neurons in a process known as **neurotransmission**. For this to happen, the drugs must first enter the bloodstream of the user. Once in the blood, the drug ultimately finds its way to the brain where it can affect neurotransmission. Users have developed several different methods to accomplish this task and are known as *routes of administration*. Some of the most popular techniques include *ingestion,* which involves eating or drinking the drug and is the primary method used for alcohol; *injection* directly in the bloodstream requires the user to inject the drug with a needle and is common for cocaine and heroin use; *smoking* occurs the when a cigarette or pipe is used to burn the drug and the subsequent smoke is inhaled (most often used for nicotine, marijuana, and crack); *snorting* occurs when the user sniffs the drug through the nose (for cocaine and similar drugs). All of these methods are successful in transporting a drug into the bloodstream, but some are more efficient than others. The blood is the final pathway for drugs before they reach the brain. Thus, routes of administration that get the drug into the blood the fastest provide the quickest "high." Drugs that are injected or smoked provide the quickest onset of effects. Injection delivers the drug directly into the blood and smoking causes a very fast absorption because the drug is transferred into the blood through capillaries in the lungs. Snorted drugs are a little slower because it takes more time for the drug to be absorbed into the blood from the nasal cavities. Drugs that are usually ingested, including alcohol, take the longest for the effects to be felt. This is because the body must digest the drug before it is finally absorbed into the bloodstream. Food can add additional time to the absorption, so alcohol's effects are felt more quickly when used on an empty stomach.

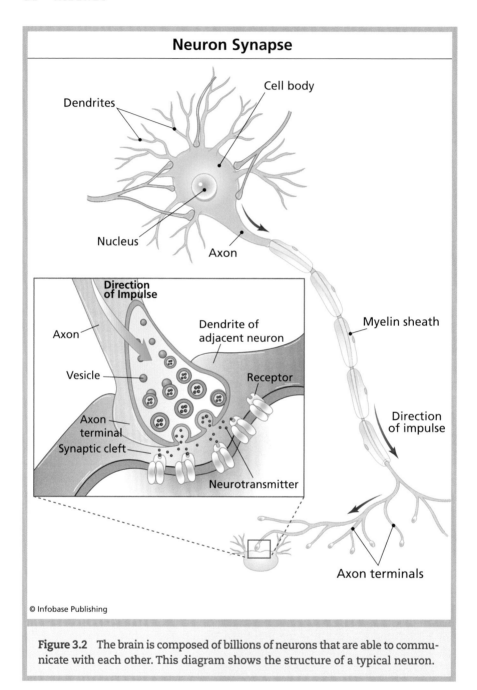

Neuron Synapse

Cell body

Dendrites

Nucleus

Axon

Direction of Impulse

Axon

Dendrite of adjacent neuron

Vesicle

Receptor

Axon terminal

Synaptic cleft

Neurotransmitter

Myelin sheath

Direction of impulse

Axon terminals

© Infobase Publishing

Figure 3.2 The brain is composed of billions of neurons that are able to communicate with each other. This diagram shows the structure of a typical neuron.

activated or to stay at rest. Like other cells, neurons have different parts—the cell body (the brain of the neuron), dendrites (that specialized area that receives the signal from other neurons), the axon (long stem that conducts the signal for communication), and the terminal body (area where the neuron releases the message to other neurons). It is very important to remember that neurons are very close to each other but not connected. Instead, there is a very small gap between them known as the synapse.

It is easiest to think of neurons as cells that have an electrical charge. This charge results from different number of electrically charged **ions** that surround the neuron. Some of these ions have a negative charge, including chloride (CL–); others have a positive charge, such as sodium (Na+) and potassium (K+). The entire neuron has a negative charge that is about –70 mV (about 1/200th the charge of a AA battery). This negative charge results from the presence of more negatively charged ions inside the neuron and more positively charged ions (particularly Na+) on the area just outside of the cell. This balance changes, however, whenever the neuron becomes activated and produces an **action potential**. An action potential is a rapid electrical shift from a negative charge to a positive charge of the neuron. There are certain ion channels, which resemble doors, located around the edge of the neuron. Whenever a neuron is stimulated, these "doors" for Na+ open up and allow it to rush to the inside of the cell. This ion brings with it a lot of positive charge and thus changes it from a negative to positive charge. This process doesn't occur in just one part of the neuron. Instead it begins at the cell body, travels down the axon, and finally arrives at the terminal body.

When this signal occurs inside the neuron, it is referred to as an *electrical* signal because there is a change in current from negative to positive. However, once the signal reaches the terminal body, the electrical signal can't move across the space to the next neuron. Instead, the signal must become *chemical* so it can move on to the next neuron. This is where neurotransmitters take over. Neurotransmitters are chemicals that carry the message from one neuron to the next. When released, these chemicals travel across the synapse and bind to the receptors on the dendrites of a neighboring neuron; they tell the neuron either to start this entire process again or to do nothing. If the process starts again, it is known as the "firing" of the neuron. Think of it like a gun being shot. It is an all-or-nothing process: One can't fire a gun halfway (it either shoots or it doesn't). Likewise with neurons, it either "fires" or it doesn't. Thus, communication among neurons is both electrical (inside the neuron) and chemical (between the neurons). This process may seem simple, but the billions of neurons that communicate with each other in different parts of the brain allow us to do very complex things like move our bodies, read, talk to others, feel emotions, understand math, play music, and feel the effects of alcohol.

NEUROTRANSMITTERS: ALCOHOL'S WEAPON

You may wonder why it is so important to understand how neurons communicate in order to understand how alcohol affects the brain. Drugs manipulate the release of neurotransmitters from neurons and thus affect how they communicate with each other. Like neurotransmitters, drugs bind to the receptors on the neuron and can either increase or slow down the release of the neurotransmitters. There are other ways in which drugs can affect neurotransmitters. For instance, once a neurotransmitter is released into the synapse, there are processes that prevent it from staying there too long. Enzymes, substances that speed up chemical reactions, break down the neurotransmitter, and transport carriers collect the neurotransmitter and move it back into the neuron. Depending on the drug, the activity of the enzymes and transporters can be either enhanced or slowed.

Drugs can also affect the activity of the neurotransmitters by regulating how often and for how long the ion channel doors stay open on the neuron. This is the way alcohol and many other depressant drugs work. Depressant drugs, including alcohol, exert most of their effects through the neurotransmitter **GABA** in various areas of the brain. GABA is called an inhibitory transmitter because it *inhibits* the activation of neurons. Whenever GABA is present, neurons are less likely to create an action potential. Whenever GABA binds to the receptor, it causes the chloride (CL–) ion door to open and allows it to enter the neuron. Chloride brings a negative charge with it and by doing so prevents the charge of the cell from becoming positive and thus no action potential is created. In other words, the neuron does not fire.

Alcohol and other depressant drugs don't directly increase the levels of GABA in the brain. Instead, alcohol works as a "teammate" of GABA and helps it do its job more efficiently, in a process known as allosteric modulation. This term "allosteric" means "at another site" and reflects the way in which alcohol doesn't bind directly to the GABA receptor to produce its effects. GABA receptors have specialized areas that allow the neurotransmitter GABA to bind and open the chloride channels. Alcohol doesn't bind to this site but instead binds at another site on the receptor and, in turn, helps GABA open the chloride door. To understand this concept, think of a dimmer switch attached to an electrical circuit. Instead of turning the electrical circuit on and off, the dimmer regulates the intensity of the circuit. Alcohol's effects as an allosteric modulator have a similar action. Alcohol regulates the intensity of the GABA effect without directly turning GABA "on" or "off." It is important to remember that in order to be a teammate of GABA and for alcohol to have an effect, GABA must be present at the receptor. In other words, alcohol can't work on its own; it needs the other teammate (GABA) there in order to do its job. The brain can also be "slowed down" by reducing the number of neuro-transmitters that usually activate or stimulate the brain. While GABA is the most abundant *inhibitory* neurotransmitter, **glutamate** is the most abundant *excitatory* neurotransmitter. Alcohol prevents glutamate from binding to its receptor and therefore decreases the chances of it activating the neuron. This is why alcohol is considered to have a "double sedative punch"—by helping GABA do its job (to inhibit the activation of neurons) while also preventing glutamate from performing its job (to activate neurons).

In order for a person to feel the effects of alcohol, this process must occur at a much greater scale than just a few neurons. There are many GABA and glutamate receptors in the brain. When alcohol is used in large enough quan-tities, it can effectively slow down certain regions of the brain to a point that they no longer function effectively. The **cerebellum** is located at the very back of the brain below the vision center. This structure is responsible for regulating coordination. Alcohol can effectively slow down functioning in this area, which is why intoxication causes a loss of coordination in the user. You've probably seen labels on alcohol (and other sedatives) that warn against driving and operating heavy machinery when using alcohol. When under the influence of alcohol, a person has more difficulty with activities that require coordination and is more likely to hurt him or herself or other people. The frontal cortex is another area that is affected by alcohol. Most people think that the brain isn't doing much whenever a person is not active; this couldn't be further from the truth. The frontal cortex inhibits or "applies the brakes" to many areas of the brain that would otherwise be active. As a result, the frontal cortex allows us to control our impulses or, in other words, have self-control. Imagine what would happen if we lost the function of the frontal cortex: We would act irrationally, lose our self control, make illogical decisions, and be unable to understand the consequences of our actions. This is very much like the behavior of someone who has been drinking because alcohol prevents the frontal cortex from functioning effectively.

Alcohol doesn't shut down every brain area that it encounters; in fact, it can also stimulate them. Just like other natural rewards, like food, water, and even other drugs, alcohol activates the **reward pathway** of the brain. Stimulation of this area makes us feel good and increases the chances that we will repeat whatever behavior caused the activation. Because food, water, and other natural reinforcers activate this area, the reward pathway helps us satisfy our basic survival needs. Alcohol's ability to activate this area, however, can be harmful to us. Within the reward system, alcohol affects more than just GABA. There are other neurotransmitters, such as dopamine and serotonin, that are changed by alcohol. **Dopamine** is a neurotransmitter that is often associated with positive emotions. Many reinforcers, like food, water, and drugs, increase the levels of dopamine within the reward system. It has been shown that alcohol increases dopamine levels in this brain area, and that it may be responsible for some of its pleasurable effects. **Serotonin** is involved in mood regulation, and levels of this neurotransmitter in the reward system are also changed when a person conumes alcohol. Changes in serotonin levels may be responsible for the depressing feelings people have during a hangover. Neurotransmitters aren't the only chemicals in the reward system that alcohol affects. Peptides have a similar function to neurotransmitters, and one of them, the **opioid** peptide, is also responsible for the pleasurable effects of alcohol. Opioids are released during many rewarding events. You may have heard of a "runner's high" after a lengthy workout. During these periods, certain opioid peptides are released, just as they are when someone consumes alcohol.

STUDYING ALCOHOL IN THE LABORATORY

How do scientists know that these brain chemicals are part of alcohol's mechanism for affecting the brain and body? Today, addiction is studied in the laboratory by modeling the disease with rodents (mostly mice and rats). These animals will *self-administer*, or give themselves, alcohol. This testing occurs in special chambers called operant boxes. These boxes have levers that, when pressed, result in an injection of the drug into the animal. The rodents have special catheters implanted into their jugular veins; when the bar is pressed, the drug is injected into the bloodstream so it can then travel to the brain. To study addiction, scientists give special compounds to the rodents that either block or enhance the activity of certain neurotransmitters. They can then measure the changes in the animals' motivation to press the bar for the drug.

Figure 3.3 The "Skinner Box" is also known as an operant box. This procedure is used to determine the rewarding effects of drugs because animals choose to receive the drug by voluntarily pressing a bar. (© *Photo Researchers, Inc.*)

This technique has been used to show that manipulation of GABA, glutamate, dopamine, serotonin, and opioid peptides can drastically change the self-administration of alcohol in rodent models of addiction.

Alcohol isn't the only drug that acts on these neurotransmitters. Almost all drugs in the depressant class can affect GABA or glutamate in some way. Because of this similarity, when depressant drugs are used in combination with each other, like alcohol and antianxiety medications like Xanax, they can each influence the effects of the other drug (a process known as drug synergism). They can combine to create an effect that is much more intense than either drug alone. This is why many sedative medications warn against taking the drug while drinking alcohol. One of the dangers of taking multiple depressant drugs together is the risk of depressing the activity of the CNS to such a high degree that the individual stops breathing.

USING THE SELF-ADMINISTRATION PROCEDURE TO STUDY ADDICTION

The self-administration model is one of the most widely used procedures in the study of drug and alcohol addiction. There are four primary reasons for its usefulness. First, it has face validity. This means that the procedure appears to accurately measure what it is intending to measure (which, in this case, is drug addiction). Addiction in humans is characterized by voluntary use of the drug rather than being forced upon them. Before the introduction of the self-administration procedure, addiction was tested in animals by forcing them to take the drug. Alcoholics are not injected with alcohol by other people because they voluntarily consume the drug. With the self-administration procedure, scientists can more accurately mimic addiction in humans by having animals show the same compulsive drug use.

Second, animals appear to self-administer drugs for their rewarding effects, because almost all of the drugs that humans abuse are self-administered by animals. Third, drug cues, objects in the environment that are repeatedly paired with drugs, are one of the main causes of relapse in humans. When addicts are presented with these cues, like drug paraphernalia, they feel a craving, or wanting, for the drug. For instance, an alcoholic who comes into contact with alcohol, or sees a picture of something that reminds him or her of alcohol, (such as a beer bottle or a particular bar), will have a strong urge to start drinking again. Using the self-administration procedure, scientists are able to pair certain stimuli, such as a light or tone, with the effects of the drug. When the animal presses the bar to get the alcohol, a light or tone is also presented and the animal begins to associate the drug with the stimuli. These stimuli then become drug cues and can be studied scientifically.

Finally, any manipulation to the animal, such as certain medications, lesions to specific brain areas, or stressful stimuli can be tested in the self-administration model to determine its usefulness in treating addiction. Some of the current medications used in the treatment of alcohol addiction were developed in studies that showed they could decrease operant responding (bar pressing) for the alcohol—presumably because the medication made the drug less rewarding.[1]

SUMMARY

This chapter has focused on the neurobiological effects of alcohol. Alcohol, like all other drugs of abuse, changes the ability of neurons to communicate with each other. It does this by manipulating the levels of certain neurotransmitters. The result is a drastic change in behavior that includes pleasurable feelings of intoxication, loss of coordination, personality changes, relief from anxiety, impaired judgment, and even blackouts. The next chapter will elaborate on this topic and explain how alcohol abuse can lead to addiction and result in permanent brain changes.

4
Alcohol and Addiction

Jonathan had become addicted to alcohol. When he first started drinking, he did so with his friends at weekend parties. Then his drinking patterns consisted of leaving work early to head to the local bar, drinking alone at home, and attempting to hide his problem from friends and family. He noticed that alcohol didn't make him feel as good as it once had, but he still found himself wanting it immensely. What Jonathan didn't know was that the years of alcohol abuse had turned into a disease. His brain had been physically changed by the onslaught of alcohol that left him compulsively to seek out and use the drug. He had become unable to control himself; instead, alcohol controlled him.

WHAT IS DRUG ADDICTION?

Drugs have been around for centuries, and some historians suggest that they are as old as man himself. The ancient Aztecs used hallucinogens that today include drugs like LSD and psilocybin (psychedelic mushrooms). Ancient philosophers used marijuana (cannabis) because they believed it helped increase their creativity, or "opened up the doors of perception." Opium, mescaline, psilocybin, alcohol, cannabis, and cocaine can be found in fresh or dried leaves, fruit, roots, barks, stems, or seeds. Thus, many of the abused drugs are found naturally in our environment. Therefore, it is not surprising that there are many opportunities to be exposed to drugs. Some individuals who take advantage of these circumstances may find themselves unable to stop using the drug. In fact, the term addiction actually means *to adhere one*

46

thing to another. In the case of alcohol addiction, the addict is bound to using alcohol and would have great difficulty stopping him or herself not only from drinking but also from *wanting* a drink.

Today, most people view addiction as a real disease and one that requires proper treatment in order for it to be successfully managed. However, drug addiction hasn't always been seen from this perspective. Just a few decades ago, the majority of the population felt that addiction was a "moral disease." This means that addicts are not strong willed enough, or lack the "mental power," to resist the temptation of drugs. Addiction, according to this view, has nothing to do with the body or brain. Instead, it is the person's "mind" that is addicted and treatment for these individuals helps them gain the moral strength to "just say no."

Our scientific community has had major advances in the technologies that have allowed for a greater understanding of just how drastically drugs can change the brain. It is now accepted that drug addiction, like many other diseases including cancer and heart disease, is a disease that has a physical, and not moral, basis.

WHAT IS ALCOHOL ADDICTION?

People often speak of being addicted to food, sports, and even the Internet. These individuals are speaking loosely about their desire for these activities. However, it would be very difficult to say that the so-called addiction to these pastimes could cause the same kind of symptoms as the all-consuming nature of alcohol and other abused drugs. Generally speaking, addiction (including alcohol addiction) is defined as the change from voluntary drug use to a state of uncontrollable drug intake despite the negative consequences (i.e., harm to self or others). One of the key points to remember about this definition is that it emphasizes that addicts have moved from taking the drug in a controlled manner or under their own free will to a state in which they can no longer control their urge to use the drug. As this chapter will explain, addicts are unable to control their use of the drug because of changes to the brain that prevent them from exercising normal levels of self-control.

Alcohol addiction is considered a mental disorder, and thus is diagnosed based on the presence of certain criteria. For instance, a family member is suspected of having an addiction to alcohol if he or she meets certain criteria

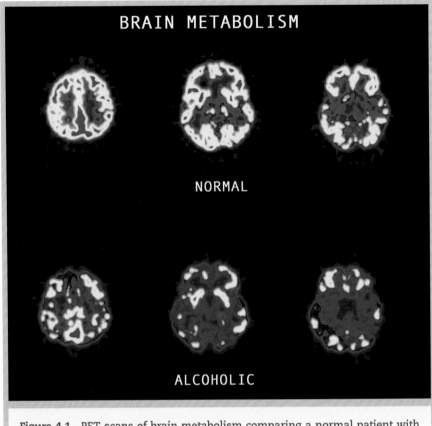

Figure 4.1 PET scans of brain metabolism comparing a normal patient with an alcoholic patient. *(© Phototake)*

for the disease. A person would be diagnosed with alcohol addiction if he or she displays at least three of the following symptoms:

1. Tolerance to the drug (after repeated use, the person has to drink more to get intoxicated than he or she is used to consuming)
2. Presence of withdrawal symptoms (certain physical characteristics of alcohol withdrawal)
3. Drinking alcohol over a longer period of time than the person originally intended
4. Unsuccessful attempts to control use despite the person's desire to quit or slow down

5. Significant amount of time spent obtaining alcohol or recovering from alcohol use

6. Neglect of job responsibilities and reduction in recreational activities in order to use alcohol

7. Continued use of alcohol despite the negative consequences associated with it

You may wonder how these criteria for alcohol addiction were established. Because drug addiction is considered a mental disorder, it is listed in the **Diagnostic and Statistical Manual of Mental Disorders (DSM)**. The current version is *DSM-IV-TR,* with IV referring to its fourth revision. It is published by the American Psychiatric Association and provides the criteria for mental disorders including alcoholism. The purpose of the manual is to allow health professionals to diagnose individuals with certain mental disorders based on the symptoms they exhibit.

For instance, if a patient went to see a doctor with symptoms of a runny nose, cough, and sore throat, the physician would probably diagnose the person with the common cold virus. In the same way, if a person goes to a mental health professional with anxiety, tremors, and mild seizures resulting from alcohol use; continued use of alcohol despite losing a job; and several unsuccessful attempts to reduce the use of alcohol, the doctor might diagnose the patient with alcoholism.

Not everyone who has a drinking problem is considered to be addicted to alcohol. Instead a person may suffer from *harmful use of alcohol* instead of *alcohol abuse* or *alcohol addiction.* These individuals have a pattern of alcohol use that damages their health (either physically or mentally), but they do not show signs of alcohol tolerance or alcohol withdrawal. People who suffer from harmful use of alcohol are often at risk of becoming alcoholics if they continue to abuse the drug and do not seek help or treatment for their disorder.

Alcoholism is not limited to a gender, race, or nationality, but rates of alcoholism differ among groups. According to the National Institute on Alcohol Abuse and Alcoholism (NIAAA), nearly 1 in every 12 adults is either addicted to the drug or suffers from alcohol abuse. The highest rates of alcoholism occur in young adults who range in age from 18 to 30, and the lowest rates occur in the elderly (over 65 years of age). Also, those who start drinking

THE DIFFERENCE BETWEEN DEPENDENCE AND ADDICTION

Unfortunately, people often confuse the terms *dependence* and *addiction,* and think they are synonymous. In fact, these words reflect two different, but very important, aspects of drug addiction. The term *dependence* is associated with *physical addiction* or *physical dependence,* while *addiction* refers to *psychological addiction.*

A user is said to have drug dependence (or physical addiction to the drug) when he or she exhibits withdrawal symptoms, the physical effects that occur when an abuser stops using the drug. The term *withdrawal* refers to the drug being *withdrawn,* or taken away, from the abuser. A user has to take the drug on multiple occasions or use a large amount of the drug for withdrawal symptoms to be experienced. Someone who is physically dependent on alcohol would show symptoms that range from anxiety to vivid hallucinations. Not everyone who tries a drug displays withdrawal symptoms.

Psychological addiction is associated more with the pleasurable effects of the drug instead of the physical withdrawal symptoms. What separates this type of addiction is that it is displayed *after* the withdrawal effects have stopped. Psychological addiction is defined as an intense wanting, or craving, to use the drug even when the user is not experiencing withdrawal symptoms. This craving for the drug can endure for months, and even years, after the addict stops using the drug. A person who is psychologically addicted to alcohol may have the urge to "fall off the wagon," or just have one or two beers, whenever he or she is exposed to alcohol-related objects in the environment (e.g., a beer bottle) without experiencing physical withdrawal symptoms (e.g., anxiety and tremors).

Scientists and mental health professionals have shown that (psychological) addiction and dependence are separate factors involved in drug abuse. A good example of the difference between the two is shown when addicts, who are treated in a rehab facility until their withdrawal symptoms have disappeared, go on to experience cravings for the drug when they are released from treatment. Some doctors, however, fail to make this distinction; addiction and dependence must be treated differently, so abusers can receive the proper treatment for their drug problem.

at an early age (around 14) are more likely to become alcoholics than someone who begins drinking at 21 years of age.

DRINKERS "AT RISK" FOR ALCOHOLISM

One of the major contributing factors to alcoholism is the amount of alcohol a person drinks. Obviously, the more someone drinks the more likely he or she is to become an alcoholic. Scientists have performed studies to determine how many people drink at levels that would put them at risk for alcoholism. According to NIAAA, approximately one-third of the United States doesn't drink at all, but about 3 in 10 adults (over the age of 18) drink at levels that put them at risk for alcoholism, liver disease, and other problems related to alcohol abuse.[1]

The amount of alcohol used is based on the number of drinks consumed, but not every alcoholic drink contains that same amount of alcohol. A "standard" alcoholic drink contains 0.6 fluid ounces or about 14 grams of "pure" alcohol. It surprises many people that a 1.5 fluid ounce shot of liquor (such as whiskey) contains the same amount of alcohol as 12 fluid ounces of beer. Thus, a person who consumes five standard drinks per week could drink either five 12 ounce beers or five 1.5 ounce shots of liquor. The table below displays some of the standard alcoholic drinks. Some have different volumes, but each contains the same amount of alcohol.

Medical professionals use the "standard drink" terminology to classify drinkers in one of the three following categories: *Current users* are those who have had at least one standard drink in the past 30 days; *binge drinkers* are those who have consumed five or more standard drinks (to reach intoxication) on at least one occasion over the past 30 days; and *heavy users* are those

Table 4.1 Alcohol in standard alcoholic beverages		
Type of Beverage	Volume of Drink	Amount of Alcohol
Beer	12 fluid ounces	14 grams
Malt Liquor	8 fluid ounces	14 grams
Wine	5 fluid ounces	14 grams
Hard Liquor (shots)	1.5 fluid ounces	14 grams

who have had five or more standard drinks on at least five different occasions in the past 30 days. Obviously, individuals who are considered binge drinkers or heavy drinkers are more likely to become alcoholics.

SHORT-TERM EFFECTS OF ALCOHOL ABUSE

When alcohol is consumed, about 20 percent of it is absorbed from the stomach into the blood while the other 80 percent is absorbed from the small intestine. The alcohol then travels in the blood to the brain where it passes the blood-brain barrier and affects the neurons in the brain. The amount of alcohol in the blood is proportional to the amount of alcohol that will affect the

SEX DIFFERENCES IN ALCOHOL'S EFFECTS

Men and women, as well as older and younger individuals, can drink the same amount of alcohol yet have different blood alcohol levels. There are two main reasons for these differences. First, there is a difference between the amount of body fat mass in men and women. Women have more adipose tissue, or more body fat mass, than men do. The consequence of this is less blood volume in women than men. Because men have more blood, alcohol is more likely to be diluted in the blood; this means that less alcohol gets into the brain. This scenario is like pouring a pollutant (alcohol) into a pool (a woman's bloodstream) versus pouring it into a lake (a man's bloodstream). Obviously, the chlorine will better cleanse the pool because the higher volume of water in the lake causes the chlorine to become diluted and, therefore, less effective. Differences in blood volume also apply to children—who have less blood than adults. For the same reason, less medication is needed to produce the desired effect in a child, and children are prescribed drugs in smaller dosages.

Another reason women are more sensitive to alcohol is the number of enzymes in their body for metabolizing, or breaking down, alcohol. Specifically, women have lower gastric levels of **alcohol dehydrogenase**. This enzyme breaks alcohol down into a substance known brain. Thus, the higher the **blood alcohol level (BAL)** the more intoxicated a person will feel. BAL is most commonly measured as the number of grams of alcohol in 100 milliliters of blood. Thus, if a person consumed enough alcohol to produce 0.08 grams of alcohol in 100 milliliters of blood, the BAL is measured as 0.08, which is considered to be legally intoxicated. The more alcohol a person consumes, the higher the amount of alcohol in the blood, and the higher the BAL.

Different levels of alcohol in the blood result in distinctive changes in behavior. While the legal limit for intoxication is 0.08, alcohol can still affect the user at lower levels. For instance, a BAL of 0.05 leads to a more easy-going and talkative person, relief from anxiety, and a few changes in personality. A

as acetaldehyde—a chemical that doesn't cause intoxication like alcohol does. Thus, with lower levels of this enzyme, women don't metabolize as much alcohol as men; consequently, more of the drug reaches the brain.[2]

Besides gender, there are other factors that contribute to differences in sensitivity to alcohol. Those who have consumed alcohol for an extended period of time have developed a tolerance to the effects of alcohol and are less sensitive to the drug. Thus, they require larger amounts of alcohol to become intoxicated. Also, the amount of food in the stomach can decrease the sensitivity to alcohol. Because alcohol must first pass through the stomach before it is absorbed into the blood, the presence of food can act like a sponge to soak up the alcohol so it can't get to the brain.

There are also differences between the sexes in what they expect to feel when they drink alcohol. Men are more likely to drink heavily when they think that it will lead to increased ability to interact with others socially. Also, if they have strong expectations that alcohol will lead to physical pleasure, they are likely to drink more. Women, on the other hand, are more likely to drink when they believe alcohol will reduce their anxiety and stress. Different expectations of how alcohol will make men and women feel results in different effects from alcohol.[3]

BAL that is higher than 0.08 results in more dramatic changes, as this level results in significant impairments in judgment and coordination. This is why the legal limit for intoxication is set to 0.08. Users with this much alcohol in their blood can seriously impair their driving ability and can endanger their life and others. Their reaction time is slowed, and their depth perception and peripheral vision are worsened. Users with this BAL may also be referred to as the "life of the party" because they can be loud and unable to control their behavior. Higher BAL levels, such as 0.15 (nearly double that of 0.08) can change behavior even more drastically. For instance, users at this level have slurred speech and major impairments in their motor functions (staggering). They may also have severe mood swings in which one moment they are happy and a few minutes later they are in tears. These individuals can also black out and have difficulty remembering events that occurred earlier. BALs of 0.30 lead to severe depression and an inability to feel sensations. The heart rate and breathing also slow during this period. Finally, a person with a BAL of 0.40 has consumed enough alcohol to become unconscious and risk death. In fact, this BAL is the lethal dose for 50% of the people who reach it.

BAL is related to the number of standard drinks a person consumes. Generally speaking, for a male weighing 150 pounds, it takes about 4 beers (12 oz each), 4 glasses of wine (5 oz each) or 4 shots (1.5 oz each) to reach the legal limit of 0.08. Interestingly, a woman who weighs the same and consumes the same amount of alcohol will have a higher BAL (about 0.10–0.12). There are several factors that contribute to BAL and these include gender, weight, previous alcohol use, amount of food in stomach, and age.

One of the main reasons people consume alcohol is for the pleasurable or euphoric effects that it produces. At relatively low BALs, alcohol can decrease worry and increase overall feelings of happiness. Intoxication is rewarding to users because alcohol increases neurotransmitters in the brain that are responsible for making us feel good. The same neurotransmitters that are released whenever we experience pleasure are released during alcohol intoxication. Because drinking alcohol is rewarding, some individuals feel they have to do it over and over, and risk becoming addicted to the drug.

The pleasurable effects of alcohol use don't last for very long, however. Soon these feelings are replaced with anxiety, restlessness, tremors, insomnia, and other symptoms that the alcohol originally reduced. When these physical signs appear, alcoholics drink to help them deal with their withdrawal symptoms instead of drinking to feel good. They begin a cycle in which they drink to feel better from withdrawal that in turn produces more withdrawal symptoms.

WITHDRAWAL FROM ALCOHOL

Alcohol withdrawal is thought of as being "opposite" to the original effects produced by alcohol. Withdrawal can be experienced during both the initial stages and late stages of alcoholism. Even people who are "social drinkers" experience some symptoms of withdrawal during a **hangover**. Withdrawal is a key part of alcohol addiction because it motivates a drinker to consume alcohol in order to relieve themselves of these symptoms.

Withdrawal from alcohol can be divided into early and late stages. The early stage of withdrawal starts anytime from a few hours to a few days after a user stops consuming alcohol. Anxiety, sleeplessness, inability to eat, tremors (sometimes referred to as the "shakes"), high blood pressure, and increased heart rate are some of the symptoms associated with this part of withdrawal. Additionally, users just "feel bad" during this stage and have a hard time finding pleasure in any activity.[4]

The late stage of withdrawal is associated with **delirium tremens (DTs)**. This consists of many symptoms—fever, irregular heartbeats, confusion, disorientation, and agitation. Some of the most notable symptoms are hallucinations. When alcoholics are experiencing DTs, they may have visual illusions of small animals like snakes, rats, insects, and even "pink elephants." The type of hallucinations depends on the environment in which the person is located. For instance, certain wallpaper designs can cause hallucinations of snakes while others may cause illusions of bats or crows. Most of these hallucinations are visual, but some alcoholics report feeling tactile sensations of things crawling on their skin. These symptoms are often accompanied by severe anxiety, panic attacks, and even paranoia. Alcoholics who suffer from DTs do not understand what is real and what is not. They must be protected from self-harm during their outbursts of irrational behavior. Obviously, it's easy to understand why this disorder is sometimes referred to as "the horrors," "the fear," and "trembling madness." If these symptoms are left untreated, nearly one-third of these alcoholics die. When this happens, death occurs from a very high fever, shock, or hyperthermia.[5]

TOLERANCE TO ALCOHOL'S EFFECTS

Tolerance to the effects of alcohol is often associated with alcohol's withdrawal symptoms. Alcohol tolerance refers to a decrease in the body's response to alcohol after repeated use of the drug. You can compare it to the way you become accustomed to a noisy neighbor's loud music. It used to bother you at first, but after being repeatedly exposed to it you become "used to," or tolerant to, the loud noise. Tolerance to alcohol works in much the same way. The first time someone uses alcohol the body responds maximally to it and the person can become intoxicated with a relatively small amount of the drug. But after repeated use, the body becomes familiar with it and responds less and less over time. As a result, the user has to drink more alcohol to feel the same effects. In other words, over time, more alcohol is required to become intoxicated.

Alcohol withdrawal symptoms become progressively worse as tolerance to alcohol increases. This is because the longer the period of alcohol use the more the body becomes accustomed to alcohol's effects. When a tolerance is built up within the user, withdrawal symptoms are more likely because the body is expecting alcohol nearly all the time. When no alcohol is present, the body still reacts as if it is and overcompensates, resulting in symptoms that are opposite of the effects of alcohol (e.g., anxiety, tremors).

There are two main ways in which the body produces alcohol tolerance. The first is by increasing the amount of alcohol dehydrogenase. This enzyme metabolizes (breaks down) alcohol within the liver and bloodstream into a nonintoxicating form. When alcohol is metabolized before it reaches the brain, the user doesn't feel as intoxicated. The second is by preventing alcohol from changing the way neurons interact. With this method, instead of being metabolized before it reaches the brain, alcohol still binds to neurons, but the neurons' reaction to this event is not "slowed down" as it used to be. These two methods differ, but both result in the abuser needing more alcohol to become intoxicated than when he or she started drinking.

LONG-TERM EFFECTS OF ALCOHOL ABUSE

The effects of alcohol on the body and brain aren't limited to intoxication and periods of alcohol withdrawal. There are some long-term consequences that result from the abuse of alcohol, most of which can cause severe changes in the body. Some such effects appear to improve with time, but others are irreversible changes that last even after alcohol use has stopped.

We'll start by exploring two of the consequences of excessive alcohol use on the brain. Alcoholics have a high risk of developing a disorder known as Wernicke's encephalopathy, which consists of a near constant state of confusion, deficits in short-term memory, loss of coordination in muscle movements, and difficulty moving the eyes. Everyone experiences confusion from time to time, but imagine yourself in a constant state of confusion that you cannot escape. Also, try to imagine meeting someone new for the first time, leaving the room for five minutes, and returning with the feeling that you are meeting the same person for the first time. This is an example of what an alcoholic who has developed this disorder might experience. Even worse, if left untreated this condition could lead to a coma or even death. Scientists have discovered that this disorder results from a lack of vitamin B1, so anyone with a severe lack of this vitamin could develop the disorder. Alcoholics are particularly at risk because alcohol prevents the absorption of this vitamin into the body. Fortunately, if detected in its early stages and treated properly, alcoholics with Wernicke's encephalopathy can recover well enough to function on their own.[6]

If Wernicke's encephalopathy is left untreated, it can develop into an even more serious disorder known as Korsakoff's psychosis. This syndrome includes severe amnesia, false memories, and loss of interest in daily activities. These patients may also display muscle tremors and difficulty with coordination. Alcoholics with this disorder experience amnesia (deficits in their memories). Like patients with Wernicke's encephalopathy, individuals suffering from this condition have trouble with short-term memories but also lose some earlier memories. In addition, they have great difficulty forming new memories. Thus, alcoholics with Korsakoff's psychosis may forget important events in their life (e.g., their own birthday, the day they met their spouse) and also be unable to form memories of events that haven't yet occurred

Alcoholic Liver Disease

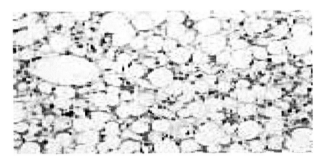

Fatty Liver

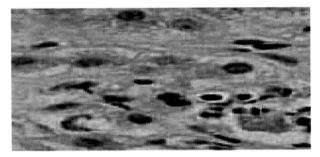

Alcoholic Hepatitis

Cirrhosis

Figure 4.2 Cirrhosis of the liver occurs after nearly a decade of heavy drinking. The liver is unable to perform its function because of the buildup of scar tissue. *(National Institute on Alcohol Abuse and Alcoholism)* (e.g., an upcoming anniversary, a special event). This disorder results from an alcoholic's lack of vitamin B1, but also from neuron loss in certain brain regions. Obviously, alcoholics with this disorder have difficulty functioning on their own and require full-time care. Treatment for this condition consists of a therapy that replaces the lack of vitamin B1. Some patients have a partial recovery from Korsakoff's psychosis, but most suffer from memory problems even after treatment.

After more than a decade of heavy drinking, alcoholics are prone to experience liver problems, most notably cirrhosis of the liver. Cirrhosis occurs because alcohol blocks the breakdown of protein, fat, and carbohydrates, and this eventually leads to an inability of the liver to function correctly. Essentially, the liver becomes covered in scar tissue and can cause serious health problems for the alcoholic.

Years of alcohol use can cause other health problems. For instance, both male and female alcoholics suffer from sexual dysfunctions. Alcoholic men suffer from erectile dysfunction (ED), low sperm count, and decreased testes

ARE THERE BENEFICIAL EFFECTS OF ALCOHOL?

There is a lot of media attention on the negative effects of heavy alcohol consumption. These effects include, but aren't limited to, memory problems, liver disease, heart disease, brain damage, and cancer of the mouth, tongue, and respiratory areas. However, scientific research has shown hat not all of alcohol's effects are negative. For instance, moderate amounts of alcohol consumption, but not heavy use or binge drinking, can benefit our cardiovascular system. Alcohol increases the levels of high-density lipoproteins (HDL) in our bodies. This is known as "good" cholesterol, which works by removing the "bad" cholesterol from our blood. It also prevents the build-up of platelets in our arteries, and this protects us from some cardiovascular diseases.

This research isn't a promotion to use alcohol, however. There are many daily activities, such as aerobic exercise, proper diet, and weight loss, that can contribute the same effects to our HDL levels as moderate amounts of alcohol consumption.

size. Alcoholic women suffer from a decrease in sexual desire, painful inter-
course, and disruptions in their menstrual cycle, and they have a higher rate
of spontaneous abortions. Alcoholism is also associated with an increase in
heart disease because it damages the muscles of the heart.[7]

FETAL ALCOHOL SPECTRUM DISORDER

Addiction to alcohol can hurt more than just the user. In fact, an alcoholic can
permanently damage the brain of a developing child, which is the case with
Fetal Alcohol Spectrum Disorder (FASD). In this disorder, a pregnant woman
exposes the fetus to heavy amounts of alcohol. The mother's consumption of
alcohol during the development of the child's brain can cause serious damage
to the organ. As a result, babies with FASD have a low IQ, stunted growth,
and distinctive facial features (e.g., wide-set eyes, lack of a groove above the
upper lip, thin upper lip, small head). Additionally, FASD is the leading cause
of mental retardation in the Western world.[8]

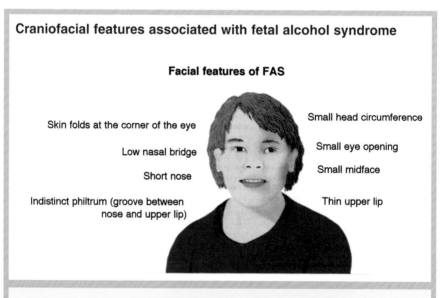

Figure 4.3 Fetal Alcohol Spectrum Disorder results from exposure to alcohol
during gestation. The mother's consumption of alcohol during pregnancy can
damage the development of the unborn child. *(National Institute on Alcohol
Abuse and Alcoholism)*

Mothers who don't drink heavy amounts of alcohol during pregnancy can still cause harm to the baby. These children may not show all of the characteristics of FASD, but still have learning, memory, and behavioral problems like hyperactivity, promiscuity, and drug addiction. These children had no control over their mother's drinking, but through no fault of their own, they have been exposed to alcohol before they were born and have to live with the consequences of it for the rest of their lives.

GENES AND ALCOHOLISM

FASD is a only one example of how alcoholism can affect those who have never taken a drink. For example, alcoholism does appear to "run in the family." This means that individuals with a parent or grandparent who suffered from the disease may have a greater risk of becoming alcoholics. This research has shown us that it's not only the amount of alcohol one drinks that determines one's risk for alcoholism, but one's DNA as well.

Some of the earliest work on this topic revealed that there was a greater rate of alcoholism among identical twins than in fraternal twins (identical twins share the same DNA, whereas fraternal twins have similar DNA to that of siblings). Much of the work in this area has used mice to determine what genes are involved in alcoholism. Scientists can use genetically manipulated mice, referred to as knockout mice, to delete certain genes from them and then measure how much they like or dislike alcohol. While scientists have yet to identify one single gene that is responsible for alcoholism, they have found a few candidates. It appears that genes regulating the production of receptors for dopamine and opioids (brain chemicals that are involved in the effects of alcohol) may reveal the genetic basis for this disorder.[9]

Many people know someone who is either an alcoholic and has a problem with abuse. If the person happens to be a parent, it can be scary for the child. Children of alcoholics are almost four times more likely to have a problem with alcohol when they are older. This statistic may seem daunting, but alcoholism isn't the only thing these kids inherit from their parents; moreover, genes are not the sole determinant of alcohol abuse. One of the most important things to remember is that an increased risk for alcoholism does not make the disorder your destiny. In fact, more than one-half of all children with alcoholic parents do not suffer from alcoholism themselves.[10]

THE BEHAVIOR OF AN ALCOHOLIC

The behavior of someone who is addicted to alcohol changes dramatically from when the person first begins drinking to the late stages of their addiction. At first he or she may drink heavily only at parties, social gatherings, or other opportunities that serve as excuses for drinking. While others at the party are drinking socially, the abuser may drink very large amounts of alcohol. Next, the abuser begins to drink at home or when alone. Less attention is paid to their family, school, and work responsibilities. More alcohol is needed for intoxication than during the earlier stages of abuse. The abuser may lie about his or her drinking or try to hide it from friends and family. Alcoholics can become angry when someone tries to discuss his or her drinking. Drinking has changed from a nighttime activity to a daily ritual that now interferes with an ability to lead a normal life. Thus, alcohol has become the focus, and every thought is centered on how the abuser will get the next drink.

Let's consider the behavior of an employee who suffers from alcohol addiction. During the early stage, the abuser drinks to relieve the pressures from work. Job stress may continue to grow and thus so does the person's use of alcohol. At this stage, the employee drinks during lunchtime and even finds excuses ("I'm not feeling well") to leave work early to head to the bar. This person's job performance has declined.[11]

During the middle stage, the abuser misses work for unlikely reasons. He or she sneaks or hides drinks at work and may show signs of withdrawal during work hours (tremors, anxiety). The person's inability to concentrate on anything but alcohol has caused a significant decrease in work productivity. He or she may leave for lunch early and not return to work afterward. This person drinks alone at the local bar. Problems with spouses and children arise. The alcoholic now take multiple days off a week to drink, but will not admit to a drinking problem.

In the final stage, the alcoholic is mostly absent from work, and generally incompetent when at work. People cannot depend on this person at all, and serious financial and family problems go unresolved. The life of the alcoholic has changed from a focus on family and work to the idea that work interferes with the ability to drink.

ALCOHOLISM AND THE BRAIN

Years of scientific research has revealed that alcoholism causes extensive changes in the brain. These changes range from near-permanent alterations in neurotransmitter levels to adaptations of entire brain structures. Regardless of the specific change, the end result is an uncontrollable desire to use alcohol regardless of the consequences that may ensue.

This book has placed a lot of emphasis on the way alcohol affects neurotransmitters. This effect of alcohol abuse is not only true during alcohol's intoxicating effects, but also during alcoholism. Drugs of abuse, including alcohol, activate the brain's reward system, including changes in dopamine and opioids (both of which help us feel pleasure). Other rewards, such as food, water, chocolate, and attractive people also activate the reward system. When this system is activated, not only does it cause pleasure, but it also focuses attention on the reward-activating object.

Although both drugs and other natural rewards activate this area of the brain, they don't do so equally. In fact, drugs activate this area of the brain much more than other rewards and essentially "highjack" the system. Levels of the neurotransmitter dopamine and opioids are elevated more during drug reward than during food and water rewards. As a result, the brain focuses even more attention on the drug. This highjacking of the reward system causes the addict to focus all of his or her attention and resources on getting more alcohol. The brain essentially "wants" the drug more than anything else. In fact, most alcoholics report that the drug make them feel less good than it used to, but they still "want" it tremendously.[12]

Alcoholism does more than just change the levels of certain neurotransmitters. Some areas of the brain that we use in everyday functions are drastically changed by alcohol addiction. Psychological addiction to alcohol causes changes in brain centers that control our pleasure, motivation, inhibitions, and memory. In other words, the addicted brain is physically different from a brain that is not addicted to alcohol.[13]

Once the brain becomes addicted, the prefrontal cortex, an area of the brain that is responsible for our self-control, is changed so that the addict becomes unable to control the desire to take the drug. An alcoholic who is told to resist an urge shows less activation in the frontal cortex than someone who is not an addict. Areas that are involved in memory, such as the amygdala and **hippocampus**, change in such a way that memories of the drug and its effects are very strong and often overwhelm the addict. An alcoholic who is shown a picture of a beer bottle or related object has much more activation in these areas of the brain than a nonalcoholic shown the same picture. An area similar to the frontal cortex, the **orbital frontal cortex**, is responsible for motivating or driving the addict to find the drug. This area of the brain is activated when one feels motivated to achieve a goal. In alcoholics, this area becomes overactive and is responsible for driving the addict's behavior toward finding and using the drug.

All of the changes in the brain result in radical changes in the behavior of the addict. A nonaddict is able to resist the urges of drugs and control his or her behavior. However, the alcoholic is plagued by strong memories of alcohol, an inability to control urges to use alcohol, and a persistent desire and motivation to find alcohol. When combined, these changes in the brain guide the addict's behavior to compulsively seek out more alcohol while ignoring other, more important aspects of life such as family and friends.

SUMMARY

This chapter has focused on alcohol addiction and included a detailed description of alcoholism and the brain changes that occur with this disease. The next chapter will discuss treatment for individuals who suffer from alcoholism. Although the brain changes that occur in alcoholics are drastic and sometimes permanent, treatment for this disease can help these individuals cope with their disorder and fight the addiction to alcohol.

5
Treatment for Alcohol Addiction

Chloe had suffered from alcoholism for many years. The disease had ruined her potential to become the lawyer she had dreamed of as a child. In addition, her family members also had to deal with the consequences of her actions. They were often paying for her car accidents, lending her money for rent, and buying her groceries. Finally, after years of alcohol abuse, Chloe entered treatment for her alcohol addiction. At first she was unwilling to admit she had a problem. However, her friends and family staged an intervention with her and told her of the pain and suffering the disease had inflicted on her and the family. Through her participation in Alcoholics Anonymous, Chloe first came to understand that alcohol addiction had physically changed her brain and she was powerless over the desire to drink. Fortunately, she has many additional treatment options, ranging from behavioral methods to prescription medications, which can help her fight the complex disease of alcoholism.

Alcoholism is a disease that damages the lives of both the user and his or her family and friends. On the surface, it may appear to be so catastrophic that controlling it is not an option. However, there are a number of treatment options available for alcoholism that range from prescription medications to group counseling. There is currently no single cure for alcoholism, but there are a number of treatments that have been shown to help alcoholics successfully manage their disease.

IDENTIFYING A PROBLEM DRINKER

One of the first steps in the treatment of alcoholism is to determine if the person in question has either an alcohol addiction or abuse problem. According to the National Institute on Alcohol Abuse and Alcoholism (NIAAA), here are several questions to consider when identifying a potential alcoholic:

1. How much alcohol does the person drink?
2. Does the user only drink at social gatherings, or also when he or she is alone?
3. Does the person drink excessive amounts of alcohol when others do not?
4. Does the individual ever become violent or angry when drinking or when confronted about his or her drinking habits?
5. Does the person drink on a daily basis?
6. Does the individual ever lie about his or her drinking habits or attempt to hide habits from friends and family?

Individuals who drink large amounts of alcohol, drink alone, become violent when intoxicated, drink on a daily basis, and attempt to hide it from others are likely to have an alcohol abuse problem. If you are more concerned about your own drinking patterns, here are a few questions to ask yourself to help determine whether you are abusing alcohol:

1. Do other people criticize your drinking and try to confront you about it?
2. Do you ever drink a lot and then feel guilty about it later?
3. Have you ever attempted to cut back on your drinking but weren't able to do so?
4. Do you have multiple hangovers per week and drink first thing when you wake up to make yourself feel better?

If you answered yes to any of these questions, then you may have a problem and might consider talking with someone about your drinking habits.

The most obvious method for helping an alcoholic is to have him or her stop drinking. Unfortunately, doing this is rarely this simple. A true alcoholic is unable to merely cut back on his or her drinking. Those who have a problem with alcohol abuse, but not addiction, may be able to decrease the amount of alcohol they consume. Cutting back is one of the most successful options, but it is not the ideal treatment for every situation. Almost every case of alcoholism is unique because different factors drive people to abuse alcohol. Additionally, there may be more than one trigger for a person's excessive drinking. If treatment is to be successful, all factors that contribute to alcoholism must be addressed in the treatment process.

The treatment of alcoholism is based on the medical model. This is the conceptualization that psychological disorders are like diseases that have symptoms, causes, and possible cures. Thus, just like any other disease, alcoholism is treated with the idea that it can be controlled, if not cured. This way of thinking has led to a variety of techniques that cover the many facets of alcoholism.[1]

Treatment for alcoholism can be divided into two categories. The first one is long-term treatment that aims either to prevent or to reduce alcohol consumption and to change the alcoholic's way of life. The other one is a more immediate treatment that arises from alcohol toxicity or poisoning. Alcohol is poisonous if taken in large enough quantities. If fact, there are about 20,000 deaths each year from alcohol overdoses. These deaths result from ignorance of alcohol's toxicity and attempts to drink excessively. Luckily, the body has a built-in safety feature that causes people either to vomit or to pass out before they consume lethal amounts of alcohol. However, some people can get around this safety mechanism by consuming unusually high concentrations in a short period time, which increases their risk of overdose.[2]

CONFRONTING AN ALCOHOLIC ABOUT TREATMENT

Often, an alcoholic will be unwilling to participate in treatment, and there are very few circumstances in which he or she will be forced to get help (such as a court order stemming from an arrest). Thus, it is likely that the addict will have to be influenced to seek treatment. Here are several guidelines provided by the NIAAA that can be used to persuade an unwilling alcoholic.

- *Stop covering up the behavior of the alcoholic.* Family members and friends usually feel sorry for alcoholics and try to make excuses for their excessive drinking. This behavior does not help the abuser because the person is unable to see the full consequences of his or her alcohol use.

- *Be specific to the alcoholic.* It's helpful to inform the user of the specific ways in which his or her drinking has hurt you, the family, and friends.
- *State the consequences.* The addict who does not seek treatment for the disease needs to understand the consequences of his or her behavior. Without making direct threats, family members should state how they will react if the alcoholic refuses help. This can include not attending public functions with the user when alcohol is present, or even moving out of the house.
- *Strength in numbers.* For the initial approach, it is easiest to confront the alcoholic when several family members and friends are present. It is even more helpful to have a health care professional present so he or she can explain the treatment options.
- *Time your intervention.* The best time to have an impact on an alcoholic is to confront the person after an alcohol-related problem has occurred, such as a verbal fight or accident. This way, the alcoholic can see the direct consequences of his or her drinking and is more likely to agree to seek help.

Once the alcoholic has agreed to get help, the particular treatment will depend on the circumstances of that particular situation. A certain technique may be successful in one situation but not in another. Thus, it is up to a mental health professional or experienced drug counselor to decide on which treatment path to pursue.

TREATMENT OPTIONS FOR ALCOHOLISM

Detoxification (also known as detox), the process by which alcoholics are immediately stopped from drinking in an attempt to cleanse the body of alcohol, is the first stage of alcohol treatment. It is accompanied by the emergence of withdrawal symptoms (see previous chapter). Detoxification is a dangerous process that should not be attempted without the help of a medical professional, as withdrawal symptoms can be fatal. While the alcoholic is being prevented from consuming alcohol, he or she often takes prescription sedative drugs, such as benzodiazepine and diazepam, which help alleviate alcohol withdrawal. Detoxification is the first part of a multistep treatment process, and by itself is not a sufficient way to treat alcoholism.

Once alcohol is cleansed from the body, the next step is to treat the patient with supplements that may help reverse some of the damage caused by alcohol abuse. Many alcoholics suffer from malnutrition and vitamin deficiencies that could be the cause of certain memory problems. Thus, treatment regimens often include vitamin supplements (particularly thiamine) and nutritious diets. Any other damage to the body, including cirrhosis of the liver or altered blood circulation must also receive medical attention before successive treatments can begin.[3]

Treatment regimens that occur after the detoxification process can be divided into either behavioral or medication treatments. Behavioral treatments include therapy-related procedures, whereas medication treatments rely on prescription drugs to reduce the desire to use alcohol.

BEHAVIORAL TREATMENTS FOR ALCOHOLISM

One of the most widely known behavioral therapies for alcoholism is **Alcoholics Anonymous (AA)**, which has been around since the early 1930s and today contains nearly 2 million members. As the name implies, alcoholics and problem drinkers are able to attend group therapy sessions without having to reveal their full name. This group argues not for a mere reduction in alcohol consumption, but instead for a complete abstinence from the drug for true alcoholics. According to AA, an alcoholic is fundamentally different from a nonalcoholic, and it is close to impossible for an alcoholic ever to drink "safe" amounts of alcohol. Therefore, an alcoholic must avoid alcohol in all circumstances.

One of the central premises of AA is that alcoholics cannot control their drinking by themselves—that they are "powerless" over alcohol. Thus, they need assistance from a "higher power" or, in other words, the God they know and understand. AA incorporates the "12-step" program, in which alcoholics advance through a series of 12 stages that include admitting one's addiction to alcohol, gaining strength through a higher power, realizing errors in the past and attempting to reconcile those errors, and living a new life without alcohol that helps others with the same disease.[4]

Figure 5.1 Alcoholics Anonymous is one of the oldest methods for the treatments for alcoholism. It provides group therapy for those who suffer from alcohol abuse. (© *Photo Researchers, Inc.*)

AA has been successful for many alcoholics and remains one of the oldest forms of treatment. However, just like other treatment paradigms, AA is not the best choice for all alcoholics. Those alcoholics who are forced into treatment, either from an arrest or accident, are not as successful in AA. Instead, AA is geared more towards those alcoholics who have made a voluntary decision to clean up their lives.

Treatments aren't limited to group therapy settings. Alcoholics can also take part in one-on-one **psychotherapy** with a counselor. In this setting, the addict can explore aspects of life that may have an influence on his or her drinking. For instance, it is common to investigate relationships with other family members or traumatic events that occurred during childhood (e.g., physical or sexual abuse). For some addicts, the opportunity to reexamine these experiences, many of which they have repressed or forgotten, results in healthier drinking habits.

Another type of behavioral treatment for alcoholism is **aversion therapy**. This technique uses both classical and operant conditioning methods in an attempt to teach alcoholics to have a "bad" memory of alcohol. In the 1970s,

SPIN-OFFS OF ALCOHOLIC ANONYMOUS

Given the success of AA, it is not surprising that other organizations have incorporated the structure of AA into their treatment regimens. For instance, Al-Anon is a program that provides assistance to the family members of an alcoholic. This group uses a modified 12-step program that focuses on problems common to family members and friends of an alcoholic. Members share their success stories and failures in dealing with loved ones who suffer from alcoholism. An emphasis is placed on how alcoholism can affect the entire family and not just the abuser. Another organization, Alateen, was specifically designed with a focus on teenagers who have a family member or friend who is an alcoholic. Teens are often unaware of the difficulties in dealing with alcoholics, and this organization can provide young people with help in understanding the complex nature of alcoholism.

some hospitals treated alcoholics by repeatedly pairing pictures of alcohol with an electric shock. Over time, the alcohol began to produce unpleasant reactions in abusers because it reminded them of the shock instead of intoxication. This type of treatment was only mildly successful and is no longer used today.

Alcoholics admit that they are vulnerable to relapse when they visit the specific environments where they used to drink. They crave the drug and are sometimes helpless against the desire to drink. A technique known as Cue Exposure Treatment (CET) aims to reduce the influence of environmental cues that signal the presence of alcohol. With this method, alcoholics are placed in a safe environment (such as a rehab facility) and exposed to various stimuli that remind them of alcohol. Initially they have difficulty resisting the urge produced by these cues, but over time they learn to control their desires, and are less likely to relapse when released from rehab.

In prison settings, inmates are rewarded for their good behavior and given tokens they can swap for rewards like extra time outside and books. A similar approach has been used for the treatment of alcoholism. Contingency Management (CM) rewards addicts for their good behavior, such as a drug-free urine test, by giving them vouchers they can exchange for rewards. Because rewards are a good way to shape the behavior of alcoholics, a technique known as Community Reinforcement Approach (CRA) focuses on those social behaviors that the addict finds rewarding. By enhancing the rewarding value of recreational activities, this technique attempts to change the lifestyle of the alcoholic so his or her focus shifts away from alcohol and toward drug-free activities instead.

Other behavioral techniques attempt to treat alcoholism by controlling, or reducing, drinking instead of completely stopping it. These techniques use counselors that teach role-playing and assertiveness methods in order to enable alcoholics to control their desire to drink in social situations. Alcoholics are vulnerable at parties or other gatherings in which alcohol is present. Through specific training, alcoholics can learn either to avoid these situations or to learn how to refuse alcohol when it is offered. Alcoholics are also likely to relapse during stressful situations, such as personal or financial problems. Thus, behavioral training can help alcoholics learn to manage their stress and find other ways to deal with the pressures of everyday life.[5]

PRESCRIPTION TREATMENTS FOR ALCOHOLISM

Medications can be used either alone or in combination with behavioral treatments. Many of the medications work by affecting the neurotransmitters involved in the action and metabolism of alcohol. One of the oldest prescription drugs used in the treatment of alcoholism is **Antabuse (disulfiram).** This drug works by preventing the enzyme acetaldehyde dehydrogenase from doing its job. This enzyme breaks down acetaldehyde into the harmless substance acetate. If it's not metabolized, a build-up of acetaldehyde is responsible for causing many symptoms of a hangover. Thus, if an alcoholic takes this medication and then drinks, the alcohol is not fully metabolized into acetate. Instead, the build-up of acetaldehyde in the body makes the alcoholic almost immediately feel the effects of a hangover. Reactions caused by this drug include headache, nausea, vomiting, throbbing of the head and neck, and breathing difficulties. This drug treatment can be particularly effective, but there is one big drawback: The addict must take the medication daily for it to be useful. This drug is often prescribed for use in an outpatient setting, and the addict is responsible for taking the drug. The alcoholic can choose simply not to take the medication if he or she wants to drink without getting sick.[6]

The medication **Revia (naltrexone)** is an opioid receptor antagonist, which means that it prevents opioids from binding to their receptors. Because many of alcohol's pleasurable effects result from the binding of opiates to their receptors, this drug can help reduce the rewarding effects of alcohol. Treatment with this drug can be divided into two stages. In the first, Revia is given to reduce the craving and desire to use alcohol. Once that stage is successfully completed, the treatment can switch to a combination of Revia and normal alcohol consumption. The purpose of this second phase is to "teach" the alcoholic that alcohol doesn't produce the pleasurable effects that it used to. This occurs because Revia is blocking the opioids and endorphins released by alcohol from binding to their respective receptors. Over time, the alcoholic will learn to not associate alcohol with the feel-good effects of intoxication.

One of the new prescription medications for alcoholics is **Campral (acamprosate).** Although the mechanism of of this drug's action is not fully understood, it appears to work by manipulating the neurotransmitters involved in alcohol's effects, primarily glutamate. This drug is used to help reduce the craving experienced by alcoholics during a withdrawal state.

Topamax (topiramate) is another drug that is thought to affect glutamate levels in alcoholism treatment. Although relatively new on the market, this prescription drug has been shown to reduce heavy drinking days in alcoholics and shows promise for future use. Another hopeful route is the use of anti-depression medications. Some of these drugs, including Prozac (fluoxetine), have been shown to decrease alcohol consumption in heavy drinkers.[7]

Sometimes, alcoholics may be given an antianxiety medication, such as a benzodiazepine or barbiturate, to help with their addiction. These drugs are given because it was once believed that many alcoholics drink because of high stress and anxiety levels. Thus, a reduction in these symptoms was thought to decrease alcohol use. However, it turns out that, although alcoholics may reduce their consumption while on these medications, it is because these drugs are substituting for alcohol. In other words, they have similar effects on the body as alcohol and can produce similar feelings. Thus, alcoholics may drink less when using these drugs, but it's not because they like alcohol less, but because they have another drug in their system that "feels" like alcohol.[8]

CONTROLLING YOUR OWN DRINKING

You may not be concerned about someone else's drinking patterns. Instead, the worry may be about yourself. If your doctor or another health professional feels that you have a problem with alcohol, the NIAAA provides several suggestions for reducing your own alcohol consumption. The first is to write down the reasons you want to stop or reduce your drinking. This might include becoming healthier or having a safer lifestyle. The next step is to set a drinking goal. Setting a goal is a great way to monitor your progress, and you can choose either to reduce your drinking or to try to avoid alcohol altogether. After that, it would be helpful to keep a "diary" of your drinking habits. You can have a chart that records when you drink the most, what types of drinks you most often consume, and where you drink most often. This information can help you identify situations where you are most vulnerable to alcohol. It is advisable not to keep alcohol in your home because even the presence of alcohol can be a temptation. You might also choose to increase your activity level. Just as boredom often leads to excessive eating, a lack of activity can promote drinking. If you feel the urge to drink, try going outside, exercising, or doing another enjoyable activity to take your mind off of

DO SAFE DRINKING LEVELS EXIST?

There is a widely held belief that in order for alcoholism to be overcome alcohol must never be used again. However, this is not true. Many alcoholics go through treatment, return to low-risk drinking levels, and never have issues with alcohol again. In fact, scientific research has shown that men can drink up to two alcoholic drinks per day (one drink per day for women) and experience very few, in any, problems with alcohol.[9] It must be stated, however, that some individuals will be unable to maintain these safe drinking levels and will eventually increase their daily use and amplify their risk of addiction or relapse.

alcohol. Finally, one of the hardest, but most effective ways to reduce alcohol use is to learn how to refuse it. This is difficult, but drinking isn't a required hobby. Just because your friends are drinking doesn't mean that you must also do so. Learning to resist the temptation of alcohol is a key step to controlling problem drinking.[10]

WHAT SIGNIFIES SUCCESSFUL TREATMENT?

How do we know if a treatment has been successful for an alcoholic? At one end of the spectrum, an alcoholic could successfully reduce his drinking to one or two drinks a week, and at the other extreme a person could remain completely abstinent from alcohol. Is the treatment of the abstinent drinker successful, and the treatment of the alcoholic who rarely drinks alcohol a failure? The answer to this question really depends on the goal of the treatment. For instance, the treatment of a heavy drinker whose goal was to stop using alcohol completely, and who shows only a slight decrease in consumption, might be considered a failure. However, the treatment of another heavy drinker who displays the same level of reduction could be considered a success if this person's goal was to stop drinking enough to keep his or her job. Thus, before treatment begins, an addict should state his or her goals specifically so he or she will have realistic expectations.

Most people assume that the best and only treatment for any alcoholic is to become completely abstinent from alcohol. This appears to make logical sense, but a "controlled drinking" goal may be more beneficial. For example, some alcoholics are less likely to enter treatment if the only goal is abstinence. Given that nearly half of the U.S. population currently uses alcohol, it can be extremely difficult for an addict to remain alcohol free at social gatherings. Finally, if abstinence is attempted several times without success, it could be advantageous for the addict to reduce drinking but not eliminate it.[11]

Another factor that contributes to the perception of treatment success is whether or not the user relapses during the treatment process. It is unwise to think that a treatment is not successful if an alcoholic "falls off the wagon" during the recovery period, as many addicts, regardless of their addiction, are likely to do so at least once. Relapse is now considered to be one of the many facets of addiction. In fact, the currently accepted definition of addiction refers to the disease as being a "chronic *relapsing* disorder." Therefore, both addicts and their friends and family should understand that relapse is part of the journey and not a failure of the treatment.

THE EFFECTS OF STEREOTYPES ON TREATMENT SUCCESS

There are several factors that can influence whether or not an alcoholic decides to enter treatment, and one of these is created by society. The general public has different stereotypes of alcoholic men and women. For instance, our society attaches less of a stigma to alcoholic men than to alcoholic women. Americans like to hear the story of the underdog who rises against the odds and becomes successful. Alcoholic men are more likely than women to be portrayed in this way. Alcoholic women, on the other hand, are more often seen as "immoral," and have a more negative stigma attached to their addiction.[12] As a result, they are less likely to admit to having a problem or seek treatment for the disease.

SUMMARY

This chapter has examined the many treatment options available for those who suffer from alcohol addiction. These treatments range from behavioral

WHERE TO GET HELP FOR
ALCOHOL ADDICTION

Alcohol has many dangerous and life-threatening effects. If you are abusing the drug, or suspect that someone you know is, it is critical to find treatment. The sooner that the abuser begins to receive treatment for the addiction, the more likely that the intervention will be successful. It is *not* true that addicts must first hit "rock bottom" before treatment can be helpful.

Numerous Web sites provide information on how and where to start the treatment process. These include the National Institute on Drug Abuse (NIDA) site and the National Institute on Alcohol Abuse and Alcoholism (NIAAA) site, which can be found at http://www.nida.nih.gov/ and http://www.niaaa.nih.gov/.

The Substance Abuse and Mental Health Services Administration (SAMHSA) is another useful Web site that provides listings for both public and private facilities in the United States that are licensed and certified to treat drug addiction. The Substance Abuse Treatment Facility Locator on their site can be found at: http://dasis3.samhsa.gov/Default.aspx

It is also helpful to contact friends and family members of the individual who is having problems with alcohol. These individuals can provide support and may also know professionals in the community who can help with the treatment process. Alcohol addiction is not an incurable disease, and like illnesses such as diabetes, hypertension, and asthma, it can be successfully treated with the proper care.

methods, including therapy and aversion techniques, to prescription medications that can reduce withdrawal symptoms and the urge to drink. Some alcoholics require multiple methods, whereas others find help with only a single treatment. Each alcohol addiction is unique, so the circumstances surrounding the addiction will determine the best treatment path to use. Success in treatment requires more than the willingness of the addict, because family members and friends are also instrumental in the recovery process.

6
Alcohol and the Law

Robbie had the type of life everyone envied. He was a very popular and intelligent young man. In high school, Robbie was one of the top athletes and had the highest grade point average in his class. His future appeared to be bright. However, when Robbie left home and went to college on a football scholarship, his life took a horrifically bad turn. He wasn't old enough to use alcohol legally, but found himself surrounded by the drug and began to drink. Soon, Robbie became known as the "life of the party" and was invited to many social gatherings. His popularity remained high, but so did his use of alcohol. After a long night of party-ing, Robbie made the unfortunate choice to get behind the wheel of a car. Alcohol had caused his attention and reflexes to weaken, and as a result Robbie hit another car in a head-on collision. Drunk driving had taken Robbie's life as well as the life of an innocent person on the same road. Accidents like this are common, but laws have been created to reduce the negative impact of alcohol on our society.

In 1984, the federal government passed legislation that created a minimum legal drinking age (MLDA) of 21 within the United States. This law made it illegal for anyone under 21 to purchase or possess alcohol. This legislation was created to reduce drinking and alcohol-related problems in youths. The government believed that severe consequences would discourage teens from drinking and also lower the number of alcohol-associated traffic fatalities. This law has been fairly successful, because from 1988 to 1995 there was a 47% decrease in alcohol-related deaths from traffic accidents. This MLDA of

21 has remained in effect since it was established, and some states have added additional laws to regulate underage drinking. These laws include punishment for using a fake ID to obtain alcohol and a minimum age for those who serve alcohol to others (e.g., a bartender or waitress).[1] Since three decades have passed since these laws were established, the question is whether or not they remain effective.

DOES THE MINIMUM DRINKING AGE SAVE LIVES?

Some people, particularly those under the legal age to drink, disapprove of the law that requires people to be 21 years of age to consume alcohol. It is argued that if someone who is 18 years old can go to war, smoke cigarettes, and attend college he or she should also be able to use alcohol legally. However, scientific research has shown that a minimum drinking age of 21 can save lives. One of the most comprehensive studies on this topic revealed that, when compared to many other factors (such as economic differences, improvements in roadways and vehicles, and lowering of the illegal BAL limit to 0.08), the MLDA of 21 had the biggest impact on deaths from alcohol-related car accidents. This study also showed that the second biggest factor in saving lives was the enforcement of strong sanctions against using a fake ID to purchase alcohol. Other studies have shown that the MLDA of 21 saves an estimated 1,000 traffic deaths each year.[2]

UNDERAGE DRINKING AND ADDICTION

The minimum drinking age of 21 wasn't set arbitrarily. It serves to protect people who are at risk for alcoholism or drinking problems. Studies have examined the age at first drink (AFD) and the subsequent risk of alcohol-use disorders (AUDs), and the findings have been very interesting. One experiment found that those individuals who started drinking before age 15 were more likely to have alcohol problems than those people who started after they were of legal age.[3] In fact, underage users are four times more likely to suffer from alcoholism when they reach adulthood.

There are several reasons why teens who use drugs are more likely to develop addiction. First, teens have an underdeveloped brains compared to adults' brains—particularly in the region that gives us self-control. Some teens can be easily encouraged to try drugs because they are more willing to take risks. Exposure to drugs at this age could alter the developing brain, making those individuals more sensitive to drugs, or could cause them to abuse drugs uncontrollably. Finally, the part of the brain that allows young people to understand the long-term consequences of their actions is not fully developed. Thus, they might not see the harm in trying alcohol or other drugs at such a young age.

Underage drinking is a widespread problem. In the United States alone there are about 10.8 million underage drinkers. Nearly three-quarters of 12th graders, more than two-thirds of 10th graders, and two in five 9th graders have consumed alcohol—more than cigarettes and marijuana combined. Thus, among adolescents, alcohol is the drug of choice. Not only do adolescents drink, but they also often engage in binge drinking. Approximately one quarter of all 11th and 12th graders have participated in drinking five or more drinks at one event. There are serious health consequences associated with underage drinking. Injury is the leading cause of death among young people in the United States, and alcohol is the leading contributor to those deaths: About 5,000 underage teens die each year from alcohol-related injuries. Among those, about 1,900 deaths result from car accidents, approximately 1,600 deaths from homicides, and about 300 from suicides each year.[4]

HOW KIDS GET ALCOHOL

Underage people can't just walk into a store and buy alcohol. Instead, they must resort to illegal means to obtain the drug. The most prevalent way teens can obtain alcohol is by having an adult buy it or give it to them. In one survey, nearly 40% of underage drinkers obtained alcohol at no cost from an adult, and 6% were given alcohol by their parents.[5] Sometimes, in an attempt to be seen as "cool," parents host drinking parties at their homes that provide free alcohol to underage teens. These parents falsely believe that having alcohol at a parent-chaperoned house provides a safe environment for drinking, but seldom are parents able to control what occurs after the party.

Less frequently, underage kids get alcohol by stealing. Many kids are caught each year trying to steal alcohol from convenience stores and liquor outlets. Parents sometimes leave alcohol in the home, and by doing so can give children another method to steal the drug. In recent years, alcohol has become available for order online. With these services, alcohol can bypass the stores and be shipped directly to the home. Although these vendors are required to check identification upon delivery, some underage kids are able to buy alcohol with this method.

COLLEGE DRINKING

Even people who can use alcohol legally may still break the law. This is especially relevant to college students, who often display rambunctious behavior while intoxicated. In addition to health consequences, college drinking also results in many individual and negative social outcomes. For instance, each year approximately 500,000 college students are unintentionally injured while under the influence of alcohol, and 100,000 students are assaulted by other students who were drinking.[6]

Many personal crimes (including injury, sexual coercion and rape, and impaired driving) are committed while people are intoxicated. Societal crimes include vandalism and damage to property, hate-related crimes and assaults, and noise disturbances. Finally, college drinking results in a tremendous cost to an academic institution. Property damage, poor town relations, and legal costs associated with student intoxication can burden the institution considerably.[7]

DRUNK DRIVING

One of the biggest problems associated with alcohol abuse is the possibility that individuals will attempt to drive after they have been drinking. Drunk driving can occur in both underage drinkers and those who are over 21. Driving drunk is also known as *driving under the influence (DUI), driving while intoxicated (DWI), and operating a vehicle under the influence (OVI).* In 2006, it was estimated that nearly 18,000 people died from alcohol-related collisions (approximately 40% of all traffic deaths in the United States), and that 275,000 people were injured in alcohol-related crashes. Drunk driving is a problem on college campuses as well. Of the 8 million college students in the United States, 25% of them drove while under the influence of alcohol, and 37% rode with a driver who was intoxicated.[8]

In the United States, all states enforce laws that are designed to reduce drunk driving by imposing severe punishment for offenders. All drivers with

Figure 6.1 Driving while under the influence of alcohol is both illegal and dangerous. Serious injury or death is possible for the driver and innocent. (© *Visuals Unlimited*)

a BAL of 0.08% (80 mg of alcohol in 100 milliliters of blood) are considered to be intoxicated and could be cited for driving under the influence. Police can determine a driver's BAL by administering the **Breathalyzer** test. This device can determine the amount of alcohol in one's blood by analyzing the alcohol content from a breath sample. When a person exhales, alcohol is present and can be quantified by this device, which oxidizes alcohol and measures the electrical current produced. Larger currents reflect higher amounts of alcohol in the blood and thus can indicate the amount of alcohol consumed.

Police can also conduct a **field sobriety test** through a behavioral evaluation of a driver's intoxication. After checking for alcohol odor, slurred speech, bloodshot eyes, and other indicators of intoxication, officers may ask the driver to perform tests that measure his or her *divided attention* capabilities. For instance, the driver may be asked to follow a moving object with his or her eyes, walk in a straight line, stand on one leg, touch a finger to the nose repeatedly, recite the alphabet, or count backwards from a particular number.

These tests allow the officer to determine if the driver has had his or her attention and motor abilities affected by alcohol. If these abilities are weakened, this indicates that the driver lacks the precise reaction skills that are necessary to operate a vehicle safely.

CHARGES FOR DRUNK DRIVING

If a driver is found guilty of driving under the influence of alcohol, there are serious repercussions. If a driver refuses to take a Breathalyzer test, most states will immediately suspend that person's license. Also, many states have a *zero tolerance* policy for individuals who are under 21 years of age. If they are caught with any amount of alcohol in their system (not just 0.08% or above), they will immediately be punished (most likely through a suspension of driving privileges). For individuals over 21 who are caught with a BAL of 0.08% or higher, they are likely to receive a driver's license suspension for a first offense. Some states also have harsher penalties if the driver is convicted of having a very high BAL, such as 0.15%, which is nearly double the legal limit. Repeat offenders are subject to longer suspension times, and even prison sentences, depending on the nature of the incident. If a driver seriously harms another person while driving drunk, he or she can be convicted of a felony DUI, be imprisoned, and have his or her driver's license revoked permanently.

THE SCIENCE OF DRUNK DRIVING

There have been many scientific experiments that investigated driving under the influence of alcohol. The ability to drive a car is diminished starting at a 0.05% BAL. The likelihood of a crash increases at this level and continues to rise as BAL level increases. When a person's BAL reaches 0.10%, the probability of being in a fatal crash is seven times more likely; and individuals with a BAL of 0.20% are 100 times more likely to have a fatal crash than those with no alcohol in their body.[9] This research supports the current legal limit set on the BAL while operating a vehicle.

Single vehicle fatalities are more likely to involve alcohol than are multiple vehicle crashes. Alcohol-related fatalities constitute a greater proportion of deaths occurring during dark hours than those occurring in daylight. Also, alcohol is involved in more crashes on the weekend than during the week.

ALCOHOL MYOPIA

You may wonder why alcohol intoxication causes people to perform risky behaviors like drunk driving. One theory that attempts to explain this behavior is known as **alcohol myopia**. This theory suggests that alcohol hampers attention and narrows perception in such a way that it causes people to react in simple ways to complex situations. Additionally, alcohol prevents drinkers from seeing the long-term consequences of their actions. Situations in life are complex, but alcohol makes people respond in straightforward ways that may not be appropriate for the situation.

Take, for instance, a situation in which a driver decides to speed after he has had a few drinks. Driving is a complicated task: A driver must know when to slow down or to speed up, and he or she must also be able to judge the distance of other cars and pedestrians. Under the influence of alcohol, the ability to make these judgments is hindered, and intoxicated users may be unable to understand the consequences of speeding or driving recklessly. The theory of alcohol myopia can also help explain why some individuals act like a "different person" when they are intoxicated. For instance, if someone were attracted to his or her best friend's significant other, in a sober state this person would probably never think of making an advance. However, while intoxicated, the user might not understand that the friendship could be ruined if he or she were to act on this desire.

Finally, although problem drinkers and people who have had multiple DUI convictions are the most likely to drive with very high BALs, almost 90% of intoxicated drivers involved in fatal car crashes are first-time DUI offenders. Thus, it appears that anyone who drinks and then drives is a threat to other people on the road.[10]

ALCOHOL'S ROLE IN OTHER CRIMES

The influence of alcohol on crime is not limited to drunk driving. Depending on the city, the number of murderers who had been drinking prior to committing a crime ranges between 36% and 70%.[11] Also, nearly 50% of murder victims are also under the influence of alcohol. Assault is another crime that is often linked to alcohol abuse, and heavy drinkers are more likely to engage in this crime. The aggressive behavior of an alcoholic is not only directed toward peers, but also toward his or her children and spouse. Sexual assault is a very personal crime that is often committed during alcohol intoxication. It is difficult to calculate an accurate number of sexual assault cases because many victims fail to report the crime. Victims fear not being believed. Many victims who do come forward report that alcohol was involved in the assault; typically, these victims indicate that both the assaulter and the victim used alcohol, but that the perpetrator consumed more.[12]

SUMMARY

This chapter has explored how alcohol can influence unlawful behavior. While alcohol in moderate levels can produce pleasurable feelings and make people more social, it can also cause people to break the law. When laws are broken, the lives of the user and others are at risk. This is especially true with drunk driving. Many people foolishly believe they can drive just as well with alcohol in their system. However, research shows that even moderate amounts of alcohol can decrease the ability to drive safely.

7
Alcohol in the Media

Shea was a pop culture fanatic. She was always up to date on the latest gossip and controversies surrounding celebrities. She idolized pop stars and secretly hoped to become a famous actress. She thought that becoming a celebrity would allow her to experience endless parties, wealth, and stardom, and that this would be the perfect life for her. What she didn't know was that pop icons are often surrounded by drugs of abuse and have easier access to them than most people do. She was astonished to learn that many of her idols had either died or suffered from alcoholism and addiction to drugs. The near limitless access to alcohol and drugs, combined with the influence of friends and "enablers," had crushed the lives of many celebrities and even caused some to leave the world too soon.

Alcohol is a very interesting drug. On the one hand, its effects on the brain help us be more talkative, less stressed, and easier to get along with. It's used in many celebratory events such as parties, graduations, and even religious ceremonies. The image of alcohol in commercials, television shows, movies, billboards, and other advertising represents it as a harmless, enjoyable drug. However, anyone who has been around it long enough understands that alcohol can be dangerous. In fact, this drug has ruined, and even taken, the lives of both celebrities and the general public.

ALCOHOL IN ADVERTISING

The presence of alcohol in the media has become common. In fact, beer commercials remain some of the most popular commercials during primetime television shows and major sporting events like the Super Bowl. According to one report, by the time a child reaches 18 years of age, he or she will have been

Figure 7.1 Beer commercials are some of the most popular and memorable on television. *(© AP Images)*

exposed to nearly 100,000 beer commercials.[1] In order for this claim to hold true, however, the child would have to observe more than 17 such advertisements per day from age 2 until 18.[2] Despite the frequency of alcohol advertising, it is doubtful that children will be exposed to that many beer commercials.

WHY IS ALCOHOL ADVERTISING HUMOROUS?

Many alcohol-related television commercials are funny and have little to do with the characteristics of the drink. If commercials are supposed to make you purchase the product, why don't alcohol companies focus on assets of the drink like the taste or cost? The reason is because advertisers use a clever trick known as classical conditioning to make the viewer associate certain emotions with their products. Classical conditioning is a form of learning in which associations are formed between two things so that one signals the presence of the other.

To understand how this process works, consider the scientific experiment of the man who discovered it. Ivan Pavlov studied the physiology of digestion by measuring changes in salivation when dogs were presented with food. During one study, though, he noticed something interesting: The dogs began to salivate when they heard the footsteps of the technician bringing the food. After repeatedly hearing the footsteps and then being given food, the dogs realized that the footsteps *signaled* the presence of food. Thus, the salivation that occurred before the food was presented prepared the dogs for dinner.

You may wonder how this type of learning benefits you. Each time you hear sound, smell an odor, or see an object that reminds you of something else (such as the smell of your favorite food), the memory associated with that stimulus is activated. Essentially, this type of learning allows you to remember meaningful events in your life so they can be recalled at a later time. Advertisers take advantage of this basic form of learning. Commercials are made meaningful by being funny, playing a hit song, or showing an attractive person in order to evoke a positive emotion in viewers. After seeing the commercial,

Alcohol-related commercials depict users as having positive characteristics. They almost never include unattractive people in their advertisements. Most of them are actors or models being paid to appear in the commercials. Men are portrayed as cool and are usually surrounded by beautiful women.

viewers are classically conditioned to think that a particular product (e.g., beer) signals a positive emotion. Thus, they begin to associate the beer with good feelings and are more likely to purchase it.

Figure 7.2   Ivan Pavlov's Classical Conditioning experiment remains one of the most influential. The learning principles discovered by Pavlov are still used by today's advertising agencies   (© *Getty Images*)

Alcohol commercials are comical. Who could forget the beer commercial that used frogs to say, "What's up?" Alcohol companies and many other advertising agencies use humor to portray an appealing product rather than one that is potentially harmful.

THE EFFECTS OF ADVERTISING ON ALCOHOL CONSUMPTION

Advertising companies are in the business of making money, so people might assume that the abundance of alcohol-related advertising would increase consumption. Numerous studies have examined the outcomes of alcohol advertising—overall abuse, increases in youth drinking, and the targeting of underage teens in advertising.

The results of these studies are mixed. For instance, one study that took place more than two decades ago found that there was no reliable basis to conclude that advertising influences nondrinkers to start drinking or for current drinkers to increase their consumption of alcohol.[3] There are similar reports during the same time period indicating that alcohol advertising has little influence on worldwide consumption of the drug. More recent reports, however, have shown contradictory results. Most of these studies have focused on the influence that alcohol advertising has on underage people. Young people are particularly drawn to the elements used in alcohol-related media, and these advertisements promote messages of positive consequences from drinking and imply that their peers drink more frequently—both of which can increase the likelihood of alcohol consumption. A number of studies have shown that alcohol advertising has a positive impact on subsequent alcohol use. For instance, youths typically view about 23 ads for alcohol per month. Each additional advertisement viewed during the month correlated to the viewer consuming 1% more alcohol. Each additional dollar spent on alcohol advertising resulted in youths drinking around 3% more alcohol. In a group of middle school children, the kids who viewed more alcohol-related commercials in seventh grade were more likely to start drinking in the eighth grade. Those youths who were exposed to more alcohol use in movies and cinema were more likely to start drinking than those who viewed less content with alcohol use. Thus, it appears that alcohol advertising does have an impact on the drinking habits of youths.[3]

ALCOHOL ADVERTISING DIRECTED TOWARD TEENS

There is a lot of controversy surrounding alcohol advertising and youths. Do alcohol companies deliberately gear their commercials to influence underage teens? What effects does this advertising have on youths? The data show that this type of advertising can influence youth drinking, but what are the ramifications? The concern is whether alcohol consumption during the teenage years can influence later drinking habits. When teens begin drinking during adolescence, they are more likely to drink as adults; this, in turn, increases their risk of becoming alcoholics or suffering from alcohol abuse. They also have higher rates of criminal activity, higher suicide and depression rates, decreased academic performance, and poor friendships. The behavior of teens who start drinking during adolescence isn't the only consequence. Excessive amounts of alcohol can lead to changes in the brain's hippocampus and impair the development of the brain. Therefore, there is a strong connection between drinking during the teenage years and damaging outcomes. If alcohol advertising actually persuades teens to drink more, then the influence of these ads could be more extensive than originally thought.[4]

CELEBRITIES AND ALCOHOLISM

Fame is associated with many things—wealth, popularity, and respect, to name a few. As celebrities gain stardom, they also gain access to many things the general public does not, including drugs of abuse. Because of their stature, celebrities are more vulnerable to addiction. They are often surrounded by drugs and have more access to them than noncelebrities. Additionally, they don't have to pay for their drugs; celebrities usually don't buy their own alcohol or other drugs.

Imagine yourself in the position of a celebrity. Thousands, maybe even millions, of people, adore you. You live a life of luxury—the most expensive cars, a mansion in Beverly Hills, and numerous people constantly around you.

Everything you do is considered "cool," and you have set trends in fashion, music, and entertainment. At the beginning of your career, you experimented with alcohol and drugs because you thought that was the cool thing to do. Use continued throughout your career, and one part of you attributes your success to the drugs. You often ask yourself, "Would I have made it this far by staying clean?" Drug and alcohol use have become part of your image; if you stopped you might lose your image as a "rebel." You don't have the same concerns as the general public because you have all the money, food, and material objects you'll ever need. One of the only thrills in your life is the feeling you get from alcohol that surrounds you wherever you go. Friends and family members drink almost as much you do because you are able to supply them with copious amounts of the drug. These individuals are known as "enablers" because they do little to stop you from using alcohol. Ultimately, your increased access to alcohol has caused you to abuse the drug to the point of alcohol addiction. The likelihood that you will admit to a drinking problem and seek treatment is low because those around you are either unwilling or unable to confront you about it. Therefore, you live in a world of alcohol that you can't escape, and it's only a matter of time until the alcohol wins.

ALCOHOLIC CELEBRITIES

Rarely do celebrities endure addiction to alcohol only; instead, they suffer from addiction to several drugs of abuse. There have been a number of high-profile people who suffered from addiction to alcohol and other drugs. Robin Williams is an actor/comedian known for his roles in the movies *Mrs. Doubtfire* and *Good Will Hunting*. Like most celebrities, Williams had a close friend, John Belushi (also a very successful comedian), who died from addiction. This caused Williams to enter rehab for his own addiction to alcohol and cocaine. Ben Affleck, who starred in the hit movies *Good Will Hunting* and *Pearl Harbor,* also suffered from addiction to alcohol and checked himself into a rehab clinic in 2001. He completed treatment and appears to be managing his alcoholism successfully. Samuel Jackson, another successful movie star, suffered from alcoholism before he made it big in the business. As is true for many addicts, alcoholism was part of his family; his father suffered from the disease. Jackson completed rehab and has since become a well-known celebrity.

Even underage movie stars have suffered from alcohol abuse. Haley Joel Osment, whose career skyrocketed with the release of *The Sixth Sense,* was involved in a car crash that resulted from alcohol intoxication. Osment was under the legal age of alcohol consumption and was ordered to attend AA meetings and an alcohol rehab program. Lindsay Lohan, star of the movies *The Parent Trap* and *Mean Girls,* has had several alcohol-related charges during the height of her career. She has been charged with driving under the influence of alcohol and other drugs multiple times and has voluntarily attended AA meetings and checked herself into rehab clinics. The ultimate outcome of her alcohol and drug problems is yet to be seen.

CELEBRITY DEATHS FROM ALCOHOLISM

Unfortunately there have been a number of well-known celebrities who have died from addiction. Sadly, their lives and careers were cut short because of their abuse of alcohol and other drugs. One of the most notable musicians to suffer this fate was the guitarist Jimi Hendrix. He was a pioneer in the guitar field and revolutionized the techniques that are common today. He was at the top of his music career for only a few short years before he overdosed on alcohol and barbiturates, causing respiratory arrest. This forced him to choke on his own vomit when he was only 27 years of age. Jim Morrison was the lead singer of the popular band The Doors. Morrison had abused alcohol for much of his career, and it is believed that his addiction contributed to his eventual heart failure. He, too, was only 27 years old. Keith Whitley was a famous country singer during the 1980s whose songs are still sung by today's popular singers. He suffered from years of alcoholism that began before he was legally able to drink. He fits the profile of a typical alcoholic because he tried to hide his drinking, often drank alone, and would devise ways to access alcohol even when his family and friends tried their best to stop him. Whitley was found lying facedown in his bed, dead from alcohol poisoning. Astonishingly, his BAL was approximately 0.48 or six times the legal limit of intoxication.

Keith Moon was the drummer for The Who, a rock band that was popular during the late 1970s and early 1980s. Moon had a destructive personality that was fueled by his addiction to alcohol. He suffered from severe alcohol withdrawal and was given a medication to help alleviate these symptoms. When he was 32 years of age, Moon ironically overdosed on the medication that was intended to help with his addiction to alcohol. John Bonham, a member the legendary rock band Led Zeppelin, is considered one of the greatest drummers of all time. Bonham was known to drink heavily. On the day he died, he drank very large amounts of vodka for breakfast and continued to drink throughout the day and into the night. When he fell asleep, he had consumed so much alcohol that his lungs accumulated with fluid, causing him to stop breathing. The American author Edgar Allan Poe is credited with the creation of several genres of popular literature. His life, however, was plagued with excessive alcohol use. The day he died, Poe was found wandering the streets completely incoherent and even wearing someone else's clothes. Although the precise cause of his death remains a mystery, many have concluded that he was suffering from delirium tremens (DTs) during the final stages of his life.

Death from alcohol can even affect those who aren't addicted to the drug. For instance, Princess Diana was the first wife of Prince Charles, the Prince of Wales. Well known for her charity work and her creation of AIDS awareness programs, she was thought of as a great humanitarian by much of the world. Tragically, in 1997, she was killed when her driver lost control of the car while under the influence of alcohol. Another celebrity, the popular late-1980s comedian Sam Kinison, was killed in 1992 when a drunk driver struck him head-on when he was driving on the interstate.

SUMMARY

Alcoholism and alcohol abuse can affect anyone. This disease may be more likely in those who have a family history of alcoholism or start drinking at an early age, but anyone who uses alcohol can suffer the consequences. This disease is not concerned with the amount of money, prestige, or popularity of the user. If fact, excesses in these areas may fuel alcohol's addictive properties.

8

Alcohol: Looking to the future

Sophia had overcome her addiction to alcohol. As a teenager, the ritual weekend drinking parties eventually turned into nightly alcohol use. She found herself unable to cope with the urge to use alcohol even though it cost her a job, boyfriend, and college education. But, Sophia was one of the lucky ones; her family and friends convinced her to enter alcohol rehabilitation. After she gained control of her addiction, Sophia was convinced that her experience with alcoholism occurred so she could understand the influence alcohol has on society. She felt the need to go back to school and research alcoholism. After graduation, Sophia worked extremely hard and became one of the top alcohol researchers in the country. Her plan is to develop a treatment for alcoholism, using genetics in order to lower the risk of the disorder in the children of alcoholics.

It should be clear now that alcohol is a drug. Just like other abused drugs (such as cocaine, methamphetamine, and nicotine), alcohol is addictive and can be potentially life threatening. Many people can enjoy the beneficial effects of alcohol without experiencing a drinking problem. There are some though who transition from voluntary drinking to an uncontrollable urge to use alcohol. The behavior of these individuals reflects the addictive potential of the drug—the one that takes lives, destroys families, harms others, disregards children, breaks the law, steals from others, and ruins potential.

ALCOHOL: PAST, PRESENT, AND FUTURE

Alcohol use is not one of the latest trends. In fact, it has been around for thousands of years and is produced by a natural chemical reaction known as fermentation. Several ancient peoples, including the Egyptians, Babylonians, and Greeks, used alcohol in many of the same ways that we do. As is true in our society, ancient cultures had different formulations of alcohol and used it in celebratory and religious events. Alcohol was highly valued in these societies, and because of this was used as a sacrifice to their gods.

Alcohol is valued in our society as well. It can be found at dinner tables each night and is a common menu item at restaurants. People demonstrated the significance of alcohol during the Prohibition era, which occurred from 1919 to 1933. During this period, the manufacture, sale, and transportation of alcohol was prohibited within the United States. However, alcohol was still greatly desired and many people found illegal ways to obtain the drug. Prohibition became widely unpopular throughout the country and was soon repealed by the government.

One of the most interesting characteristics of alcohol is its legality. Nearly anyone who is 21 years of age or older can legally purchase and consume alcohol. This is not true of most other drugs except nicotine, for which the minimum age to purchase is 18 in most states. Since alcohol is the most widely abused drug in the world but also one of the most damaging, it is difficult to understand why it is not listed on the Controlled Substances Act in the United States.

Like other abused drugs, alcohol produces its effects by altering the flow in the brain of chemicals known as neurotransmitters. Excessive use of the drug can result in alcohol addiction, and many scientists today believe that alcoholism is the consequence of alcohol-induced changes in the brain. These brain changes cause the abuser to experience cravings for alcohol and an uncontrollable urge to use the drug. Alcohol use becomes almost like a bad habit that cannot be controlled. Addiction to alcohol can also cause severe health consequences. Korsakoff's psychosis results from years of heavy alcohol use and is associated with memory deficits and neuron loss. Heavy alcohol use can also cause heart disease, cancer of the mouth and throat, and sexual dysfunctions. Withdrawal from alcohol can cause vivid hallucinations, or perceptions of things that aren't actually there.

Fortunately, there are numerous treatment options available for those who suffer from alcoholism. One of the most established treatment methods is Alcoholics Anonymous (AA). This is a group therapy technique that treats alcoholism by having the addict acknowledge that he or she is powerless over the influence of alcohol and must remove all of it from his or her life. AA also incorporates a 12-step program that enables the alcoholic to progressively help him or herself and others who have been harmed by the addiction. Treatment of alcoholism also includes prescription medications. Almost all of these medications provide relief from the symptoms associated with alcohol withdrawal or the craving for alcohol that can occur long after detoxification. The most successful treatments for this disorder are those that incorporate both behavioral and prescription methods for recovery. However, scientists and researchers are always developing new ways to combat alcoholism.

THE FUTURE OF ALCOHOL ADDICTION TREATMENT

Technology is becoming more complex with each year and scientists are developing state-of-the-art techniques to treat alcoholism. In the future, alcoholism treatment will introduce gene techniques to help individuals who suffer from alcoholism or have a family history of the disease. Currently, researchers are able to change the genetic makeup of mice and rats and observe the changes in their alcohol consumption. This type of research is used on rodents with a technique known as a *viral vector*. This is a virus that is injected into the animal to activate or deactivate a specific gene in the nervous system. This approach could be useful because it would allow scientists to put the virus in a mouse addicted to alcohol, which would turn on or off a particular gene known to be involved in alcoholism, and possibly make the mouse no longer like alcohol. As this type of research develops, it could provide an innovative way to treat alcoholism in humans.

Future treatments of alcoholism and alcohol abuse may also include the use of vaccinations. Although current drug therapy is used to prevent the craving and withdrawal symptoms of alcohol, vaccinations may ultimately provide the opportunity to treat the effects of alcohol before they even reach the brain. With this technique, scientists could block or inactivate alcohol before it can produce its effects on the central nervous system. Vaccines can make antibodies to alcohol that would prevent the "high" that comes from being intoxicated and therefore could remove the incentive to use alcohol and possibly prevent addiction from occurring.

CAN ALCOHOL ADDICTION BE UNLEARNED OR FORGOTTEN?

Through years of scientific research we now know that alcoholism results from changes in the brain. These changes are possible because the brain is able to adapt itself under certain conditions. The brain can adjust the number of neurotransmitter receptors, the number of connections between neurons, and even the pathways between brain structures. This ability is known as "plasticity." When someone experiences something new, changes occur in certain neurotransmitter receptors and synapses. Scientists believe that this process underlies our ability to learn. The brain's ability to store memories works in the same way.

Repeated use of alcohol and other drugs of abuse also cause the brain to adapt. In fact, drugs cause changes in the same brain areas that are responsible for learning and memory. Therefore, many scientists believe that addiction results from long-lasting changes in the brain that are similar to those that occur with learning. Addicts form associations between objects in the environment and the effects produced by the drug. Through learning mechanisms, these associations can become overly strong and motivate the behavior of the addict to look for drugs. Currently, scientists are looking for ways to counteract and normalize the changes that are caused by drugs. Furthermore, when a memory is activated it becomes *malleable*, or able to be changed. Scientists are trying to develop methods that can alter the drug memories of addicts when they are recalled. Thus, in the future it may be possible "unlearn" or "forget" the associations that addicts form between drugs and the environment, and this innovation could provide a revolutionary way to treat alcohol and drug addiction.

SUMMARY

The purpose of this book was to explore the many components of alcohol in society. Even though alcohol is legal, it still has the characteristics of an addictive drug. Alcohol can sometimes be beneficial to those who can control their use, but the results for people who abuse alcohol can be disastrous. There is help for those who suffer from alcohol addiction, and recent breakthroughs in the fields of neuroscience, biology, and genetics provide exciting opportunities for the development of cutting-edge treatments in the near future.

Notes

Chapter 1

1. H. L. Wagner, *Alcohol (Drugs: The Straight Facts)*, ed. D. J. Triggle. New York: Chelsea House, 2003.
2. G. F. Koob and M. L. Le Moal, "Alcohol," in *Neurobiology of Addiction, ed.* G. F. Koob and M. L. Le Moal (New York: Academic Press, 2006).
3. O. Ray and C. Ksir, "Alcohol in the Body," in *Drugs, Society, and Human Behavior* (New York: McGraw-Hill, 2004).
4. H. Yi et al., "Trends in Alcohol-Related Fatal Traffic Crashes," in *10th Special Report to the U.S. Congress on Alcohol and Health: Highlights from Current Research* (Bethesda: National Institute on Alcohol Abuse and Alcoholism, 2000).
5. J. T. Gass, *Quaalude (Drugs: The Straight Facts)*, ed. D. J. Triggle (New York: Chelsea House, 2008).

Chapter 2

1. W. A. McKim, "Alcohol," in *Drugs and Behavior* (Upper Saddle River, N.J.: Prentice Hall, 2000).
2. D. J. Hanson, *Preventing Alcohol Abuse: Alcohol, Culture, and Control* (Westport, Conn.: Praeger, 1995); W. A. McKim, "Alcohol," in *Drugs and Behavior* (Upper Saddle River, N.J.: Prentice Hall, 2000).
3. Ibid.
4. Ibid.
5. O. Ray and C. Ksir, "Alcohol in the Body," in *Drugs, Society, and Human Behavior* (New York: McGraw-Hill, 2004).
6. Ibid.
7. H. L. Wagner, *Alcohol (Drugs: The Straight Facts)*, ed. D. J. Triggle (New York: Chelsea House, 2003).
8. H. R. White, "Sociology," in *Recent Developments in Alcoholism* (New York: Plenum Press, 1993); O. Ray and C. Ksir, "Alcohol in the Body," in *Drugs, Society, and Human Behavior* (New York: McGraw-Hill, 2004); H. L. Wagner, *Alcohol (Drugs: The Straight Facts)*, ed. D. J.

Triggle (New York: Chelsea House, 2003).

9. G. D. Williams et al., "Surveillance Report #27. Apparent Per Capita Alcohol Consumption: National, State, and Regional Trends, 1977–1991," (Rockville, Md.: Nation Institute on Alcohol Abuse and Alcoholism, 1993); W. A. McKim, "Alcohol," in *Drugs and Behavior* (Upper Saddle River, N.J.: Prentice Hall, 2000).

10. O. Ray and C. Ksir, "Alcohol in the Body," in *Drugs, Society, and Human Behavior* (New York: McGraw-Hill, 2004).

11. N. E. Lakins et al., "Surveillance Report #85: Apparent Per Capita Alcohol Consumption: National, State, and Regional Trends, 1970–2006." (Bethesda, Md.: National Institute on Alcohol Abuse and Alcoholism, 2008).

12. National Institute on Alcohol Abuse and Alcoholism (NIAAA), "Total Per Capita Alcohol Consumption in Gallons of Ethanol by State, United States, 2006," http://www.niaaa.nih.gov/ Resources/Graphics Gallery/ consfigs4text.htm (accessed March 4, 2010).

13. Substance Abuse and Mental Health Services Administration (SAMHSA), "Results from the 2002 National Survey on Drug Use and Health: National Findings," in *NHSDA Series H-22*. http://www.oas. samhsa.gov/nhsda/2k2nsduh/ results/2k2Results.htm (accessed March 4, 2010); B. F. Grant et al., "The 12-Month Prevalence and Trends in DSM-IV Alcohol Abuse and Dependence: United States, 1991–1992 and 2001–2002." *Drug Alcohol Depend* 74, no. 3 (2004): 223–234.

14. O. Ray and C. Ksir, "Alcohol in the Body," in *Drugs, Society, and Human Behavior* (New York: McGraw-Hill, 2004).

15. P. E. Greenbaum et al., "Variation in the Drinking Trajectories of Freshmen College Students," *Journal of Consulting and Clinical Psychology* 73, no. 2 (2005): 229–238.

16. O. Ray and C. Ksir, "Alcohol in the Body," in *Drugs, Society, and Human Behavior* (New York: McGraw-Hill, 2004); L. D. Johnston et al., "Monitoring the Future, National Survey Results on Drug Use, 1975–2007." http://monitoringthe future.org (accessed March 4, 2010).

17. L. D. Johnston et al., "Monitoring the Future, National Survey

Results on Drug Use, 1975–2007." http://monitoringthe future.org (accessed March 4, 2010).

18. R. Hingson, "Magnitude of Alcohol-Related Mortality and Morbidity among U.S. College Students Ages 18–24: Changes from 1998 to 2001," in *Annual Review of Public Health* (2005): 259–279; R. C. Engs et al., "The Drinking Patterns and Problems of a National Sample of College Students, 1994," *Journal of Alcohol and Drug Education* 41, no. 3 (1996): 13–33.

Chapter 3

1. J. T. Gass, *Quaalude (Drugs: The Straight Facts)*, ed. D.J. Triggle (New York: Chelsea House, 2008).

Chapter 4

1. NIAAA, "Rethinking Drinking," in *NIH Publication 09-3770*, 2009.

2. M. Frezza et al., "High Blood Alcohol Levels in Women. The Role of Decreased Gastric Alcohol Dehydrogenase Activity and First-Pass Metabolism," *New England Journal of Medicine* 322, no. 2 (1990): 95–99.

3. O. Ray and C. Ksir, "Alcohol in the Body," in *Drugs, Society, and Human Behavior* (New York: McGraw-Hill, 2004).

4. D. B. Goldstein, *Pharmacology of Alcohol* (New York: Oxford, 1983).

5. O. Ray and C. Ksir, "Alcohol in the Body," in *Drugs, Society, and Human Behavior* (New York: McGraw-Hill, 2004).

6. G. F. Koob and M. L. Le Moal, "Alcohol," in *Neurobiology of Addiction* (New York: Academic Press, 2006).

7. H. I. Wright et al., "Effects of Alcohol on the Male Reproductive System," *Alcohol Health and Research World* 15 (1991): 110–114; S. S. Covington and J. Kohen, "Women, Alcohol, and Sexuality," *Advances in Alcohol & Substance Abuse* 4, no. 1 (1984): 41–56; J. N. Hugues et al., "Hypothalamo-Pituitary Ovarian Function in Thirty-One Women with Chronic Alcoholism." *Clinical Endocrinology (Oxford)* 12, no. 6 (1980): 543–551.; M. R. Piano, "Alcoholic Cardiomyopathy: Incidence, Clinical Characteristics, and Pathophysiology," *Chest* 121, no. 5 (2002): 1638–1650.

8. E. L. Abel and R. J. Sokol, "Incidence of Fetal Alcohol Syndrome and Economic Impact of FAS-Related

Anomalies," *Drug and Alcohol Dependence* 19, no. 1 (1987): 51–70.

9. R. W. Pickens et al., "Heterogeneity in the Inheritance of Alcoholism: A Study of Male and Female Twins," *Archives of General Psychiatry* 48, no. 1 (1991): 19–28.

10. NIAAA, "A Family History of Alcoholism: Are You at Risk?" in *NIH Publication 03-5340,* 2005.

11. S. Cline, "Alcohol and Drugs at Work," (Chicago: Drug Abuse Council, 1975).

12. T. E. Robinson and K. C. Berridge, "The Neural Basis of Drug Craving: An Incentive-Sensitization Theory of Addiction," *Brain Research Reviews* 18, no. 3 (1993): 247–291.

13. R. D. Baler and N. D. Volkow, "Drug Addiction: The Neurobiology of Disrupted Self-Control," *Trends in Molecular Medicine* 12, no. 12 (2006): 559–566.

Chapter 5

1. D. L. Schacter et al., "Psychological Disorders," in *Psychology* (New York: Worth, 2009).

2. D. L. Hoyert et al., "Deaths: Final Data for 1997," in *National Vital Statistics Reports,* 1999; W. A. McKim, "Alcohol," in *Drugs and Behavior* (Upper Saddle River, N.J.: Prentice Hall, 2000).

3. O. Ray and C. Ksir, "Alcohol in the Body," in *Drugs, Society, and Human Behavior* (New York: McGraw-Hill, 2004).

4. W. A. McKim, "Alcohol," in *Drugs and Behavior* (Upper Saddle River, N.J.: Prentice Hall, 2000).

5. Ibid.

6. O. Ray and C. Ksir, "Alcohol in the Body," in *Drugs, Society, and Human Behavior* (New York: McGraw-Hill, 2004).

7. B. A. Johnson et al., "Topiramate for Treating Alcohol Dependence: A Randomized Controlled Trial," *Journal of the American Medical Association* 298, no. 14 (2007): 1641–1651; D. A. Gorelick,. "Pharmacological Treatment," in *Recent Developments in Alcoholism,* ed. M. Galanter (New York: Plenum, 1993), 413–427.

8. W. A. McKim, "Alcohol," in *Drugs and Behavior* (Upper Saddle River, N.J.: Prentice Hall, 2000).

9. NIAAA, "FAQ for the General Public," http://www.niaaa.nih.gov/FAQs/General-English/default.htm#groups (accessed March 4, 2010).

10. NIAAA, "How to Cut Down on Your Drinking," in *NIH Publication 96-3770*. Bethesda: National Institute of Health, 1996.

11. O. Ray and C. Ksir, "Alcohol in the Body," in *Drugs, Society, and Human Behavior* (New York: McGraw-Hill, 2004).

12. S. B. Blume, "Alcoholism in Women," *Harvard Mental Health Letter* 14, no. 9 (1998): 5–7.

Chapter 6

1. National Center for Statistics and Analysis, "Fatality Analysis Reporting System (FARS)," National Highway Traffic Safety Administration, *www-fars.nhtsa.dot.gov* (accessed March 4, 2010); J. C. Fell et al., "The Relationship of Underage Drinking Laws to Reductions in Drinking Drivers in Fatal Crashes in the United States," *Accident Analysis and Prevention* 40, no. 4 (2008): 1430–1440.

2. Ibid.

3. D. A. Dawson et al., "Transitions in and out of Alcohol Use Disorders: Their Associations with Conditional Changes in Quality of Life over a 3-Year Follow-up Interval," *Alcohol and Alcoholism* 44, no. 1 (2009): 84–92.

4. NIAAA, "FAQ for the General Public," http://www.niaaa.nih.gov/FAQs/General-English/default.htm#groups (accessed March 4, 2010); L. D. Johnston et al., "Monitoring the Future, National Survey Results on Drug Use, 1975–2007," http://monitoringthefuture.org (accessed March 4, 2010); U.S. Department of Health and Human Services, "The Surgeon General's Call to Action to Prevent and Reduce Underage Drinking," Office of the Surgeon General, http://www.surgeongeneral.gov/topics/underagedrinking/calltoaction.pdf (accessed March 4, 2010).

5. SAMHSA, "Results from the 2002 National Survey on Drug Use and Health: National Findings," http://www.oas.samhsa.gov/nhsda/2k2nsduh/results/2k2Results.htm (accessed March 4, 2010).

6. H. W. Perkins, "Surveying the Damage: A Review of Research on Consequences of Alcohol Misuse in College Populations," *Journal of Studies on Alcohol Supplement*, no. 14 (2002): 91–100.

7. Ibid.

8. R. Hingson, "Magnitude of Alcohol-Related Mortality and Morbidity among U.S. College

Students Ages 18–24: Changes Rom 1998 to 2001," in *Annual Review of Public Health,* 2005: 259–279.

9. Organization for Economic Co-operation and Development, "Road Research: New Research on the Role of Alcohol and Drugs in Road Accidents," 1978.

10. Organization for Economic Co-operation and Development, "Road Research: New Research on the Role of Alcohol and Drugs in Road Accidents," 1978; O. Ray and C. Ksir, "Alcohol in the Body," in *Drugs, Society, and Human Behavior* (New York: McGraw-Hill, 2004).

11. K. Pernane, *Alcohol in Human Violence* (New York: Guilford Press, 1991).

12. A. S. Linsky et al., "Social Stress, Normative Constraints and Alcohol Problems in American States," *Social Science & Medicine* 24, no. 10 (1987): 875–883; A. Abbe et al., "Alcohol's Role in Sexual Assault," in *Drug and Alcohol Abuse Reviews; Volume 5 Addictive Behaviors in Women,* ed. R. R. Watson (Totowa, N.J.: Humana Press, 1994) 97–123.

Chapter 7

1. M. Oberst, "Alcohol Use Among Teens Is Epidemic in Oregon," *The Oregonian,* April 7, 2004.

2. D. J. Hanson, "Alcohol Problems & Solutions," http://www2. potsdam.edu/hansondj/In TheNews/UnderageDrinking/ 1083346877.html (accessed March 4, 2010).

3. C. T. Crawford and W. L. K. Gramm, "Omnibus Petition for Regulation of Unfair and Deceptive Alcoholic Beverage Advertising and Marketing Practices," ed. Federal Trade Commission, Docket No. 209–246 (Washington, D.C., 1985); P. Anderson, "Is It Time to Ban Alcohol Advertising?" *Clinical Medicine* 9, no. 2 (2009): 121–124; L. B. Snyder et al., "Effects of Alcohol Advertising Exposure on Drinking Among Youth," *Archives of Pediatric & Adolescent Medicine* 160, no. 1 (2006): 18–24; A. W Stacy et al., "Exposure to Televised Alcohol Ads and Subsequent Adolescent Alcohol Use," *American Journal of Health Behavior* 28, no. 6 (2004): 498–509; J. D. Sargent et al., "Alcohol Use in Motion Pictures and Its Relation with Early-Onset Teen Drinking," *Journal of Studies on Alcohol and Drugs* 67, no. 1 (2006): 54–65.

4. M. D. De Bellis et al., "Hippocampal Volume in Adolescent-Onset Alcohol Use Disorders," *American Journal of Psychiatry*

157 (2000): 737–744; C. T. Crawford and W. L. K. Gramm, "Omnibus Petition for Regulation of Unfair and Deceptive Alcoholic Beverage Advertising and Marketing Practices," ed. Federal Trade Commission, Docket No. 209–246 (Washington, D.C., 1985).

Glossary

action potential   A rapid change in the charge of a neuron; method by which neurons communicate with each other.

alcohol   Any compound that contains a hydroxyl group bound to an alkyl group.

alcohol addiction   The persistent urge to use alcohol despite negative consequences that results from excessive use of the drug.

alcohol dehydrogenase   Enzyme in the body that metabolizes (breaks down) alcohol.

alcohol myopia   Theory suggesting that alcohol lessens attention and narrows perception.

Alcoholics Anonymous (AA)   Organization in which alcoholics can anonymously admit that they have a drinking problem and receive group counseling.

amygdala   Structure located in the medial temporal lobe of the brain that regulates emotions; particularly fear and aggression.

Antabuse (disulfiram)   Medication used for the treatment of alcoholism that prevents the breakdown of acetaldehyde in the body resulting in hangover-like symptoms.

anxiety   An emotional state associated with fear and worry.

aversion therapy   Technique used for the treatment of alcoholism, by which unpleasant associations are formed with alcohol.

beer   Alcoholic beverage containing 3–6% alcohol produced from the fermentation of starches.

blood alcohol level (BAL)   Measurement used to determine the amount of alcohol in one's blood; higher BALs result in greater intoxication.

Breathalyzer   Device used to detect the amount of alcohol in the body by analyzing a breath sample.

brewery   Facility used in the production of beer.

Campral (acamprosate)   Medication used in alcoholism that reduces the desire to consume alcohol.

central nervous system (CNS)   System of the body containing the brain and spinal cord.

cerebellum   Part of the brain that controls coordination and some muscle movements.

champagne   Alcoholic beverage that resembles white wine and has carbonation added.

convulsion   Medical condition similar to a seizure.

delirium tremens (DTs)   Stage of alcohol withdrawal that includes hallucinations, fever, and confusion.

depressant   Type of drug that slows down the activity of the central nervous system.

detoxification   Process by which alcohol is removed from the body by preventing consumption.

***Diagnostic and Statistical Manual of Mental Disorders* (DSM)**   Manual used by mental health professionals to diagnose mental disorders.

disorientation   Disruptions in a person's sense of time and place.

distillation   Process by which alcohol beverages are produced by boiling and condensing the liquid, resulting in higher alcohol content compared to fermentation techniques.

dopamine   Neurotransmitter often associated with positive emotions.

ethanol   Psychoactive drug used as a beverage; ethyl/grain alcohol.

fermentation   Process by which alcohol and carbon dioxide are produced from glucose.

Fetal Alcohol Spectrum Disorder (FASD)   Cognitive and behavior disorder resulting from alcohol exposure during development.

field sobriety test   Behavioral test used to determine deficits in motor ability and attention from alcohol intoxication.

frontal lobe   Located in the front of the brain, the area responsible for motor movements, speech production, inhibition, decision-making, and many other "higher" cognitive processes.

GABA   The most abundant inhibitory neurotransmitter.

gastric   Term used to refer to the areas of stomach.

gin   A colorless alcoholic beverage produced from distillation and flavored with juniper berries.

glutamate   The most abundant excitatory neurotransmitter.

hallucination   A perception in any sensory modality (such as visual or auditory) in the absence of an external stimulus.

hangover   Period after heavy alcohol consumption that includes symptoms of dehydration, headaches, nausea, thirst, dysphoria, and other withdrawal-like characteristics.

hippocampus   Area of the brain that is responsible for many aspects of memory.

ion   Electrically charged atom or molecule.

isopropyl   Form of alcohol often used as a cleaning agent; rubbing alcohol.

Korsakoff's psychosis   Condition resulting from long-term alcoholism and that includes severe memory problems.

mead   Alcoholic beverage made from honey that was popular in ancient cultures.

methanol   Form of alcohol used as a laboratory solvent; wood alcohol.

Mothers Against Drunk Driving (MADD)   Organization that promotes efforts to reduce drunk driving and help those who have been affected by it.

neurological disorder   Disorder associated with deficits in the brain and/or mind that result in behavior changes.

neuron   Cell located in the central nervous stem that can communicate with other neurons via an electrical and chemical signal.

neurotransmission   Process that involves transmitting a signal via neurotransmitters across the synapse.

occipital lobe   Area of the brain that contains the visual cortex and regulates vision.

opioid   Chemical that binds to opiate receptors and provides pain relief.

orbital frontal cortex   Area of the brain that helps control motivation and drive.

organized crime   Often referred to as the Mafia, a network made up of criminals that engage in illegal activities for money.

Osiris   God believed by the ancient Egyptians to have invented alcohol.

parietal lobe   "Association" area of the brain the integrates the many different sensory modalities; contains area responsible for sensation.

physical dependence   Addiction to a drug defined by the presence of withdrawal symptoms.

Prohibition   Period from 1919 to 1933 during which it was illegal to produce or sell alcohol for consumption within the United States.

psychological dependence   Addiction to a drug defined by the presence of craving for the drug after withdrawal symptoms have disappeared.

psychotherapy   Technique used by therapists who explore unconscious motives that affect our behavior.

Revia (naltrexone)   Medication used for alcoholism that decreases the pleasurable effects of alcohol.

reward pathway   Consists of several brain areas that are activated when reward or reinforcement is experienced.

rum   Alcoholic beverage produced from sugarcane through distillation and fermentation

serotonin   Neurotransmitter that helps regulate mood.

Students Against Destructive Decisions (SADD)   Organization focused on the prevention of drug and alcohol abuse among teenagers.

temperance   The act of refraining from overindulgence in activities (notably alcohol use).

Temperance Movement   Organized movement during the early 1800s in the United States that argued for a reduction in, but not complete abstinence from, the consumption of alcohol.

temporal lobe   Area of the brain located near the temple that houses the auditory cortex.

Wernicke's encephalopathy   Stage of alcohol withdrawal that includes severe confusion and memory problems.

whiskey   Alcoholic beverage, such as bourbon, produced from distillation of grain mash.

willpower   The ability to resist urge; self-discipline.

wine   Alcoholic beverage produced from the fermentation of grapes.

withdrawal symptoms   Physical symptoms that occur after the sudden discontinued use of a drug.

Further Resources

Related Books

Hoffman, J., and S. Froemke. *Addiction: Why Can't They Just Stop?* New York: Rodale Press, 2007.

Oakley, R., and C. Ksir. *Drugs, Society, and Human Behavior.* 3d ed. St. Louis, Mo.: C. V. Mosby, 1983.

Wagner, H. L. *Alcohol.* Philadelphia: Chelsea House, 2003.

Web Sites

AddictionSearch.com
http://www.addictionsearch.com

The National Institute on Alcohol Abuse and Alcoholism
http://www.niaaa.nih.gov

The National Institute on Drug Abuse
http://www.nida.nih.gov

NIDA for Teens
http://teens.drugabuse.gov

The Partnership for a Drug-Free America
http://www.drugfree.org

U.S. Drug Enforcement Administration
http://www.usdoj.gov/dea/index.htm

Index

About the Author

Justin T. Gass received his bachelor's degree in psychology from East Tennessee State University. His graduate work was in the field of neuroscience, and he received his Ph.D. from the University of South Carolina, Columbia. He is currently a postdoctoral fellow in the Center for Drug and Alcohol Programs at the Medical University of South Carolina, Charleston, where his research in the field of drug addiction is supported by a grant from the National Institute on Alcohol Abuse and Alcoholism. Dr. Gass is also an adjunct faculty member in the Department of Psychology at the College of Charleston.

About the Consulting Editor

Consulting editor **David J. Triggle, Ph.D.**, is a SUNY Distinguished Professor and the University Professor at the State University of New York at Buffalo. These are the two highest academic ranks of the university. Professor Triggle received his education in the United Kingdom with a Ph.D. degree in chemistry at the University of Hull. Following post-doctoral fellowships at the University of Ottawa (Canada) and the University of London (United Kingdom) he assumed a position in the School of Pharmacy at the University at Buffalo. He served as chairman of the Department of Biochemical Pharmacology from 1971 to 1985 and as Dean of the School of Pharmacy from 1985 to 1995. From 1996 to 2001 he served as Dean of the Graduate School and from 1999 to 2001 was also the University Provost. He is currently the University Professor, in which capacity he teaches bioethics and science policy, and is President of the Center for Inquiry Institute, a think tank located in Amherst, New York and devoted to issues around the public understanding of science. In the latter respect he is a major contributor to the online M.Ed. program—"Science and The Public"—in the Graduate School of Education and The Center for Inquiry.